READING and DATING
ROMAN IMPERIAL COINS

by
ZANDER H. KLAWANS

FOURTH EDITION

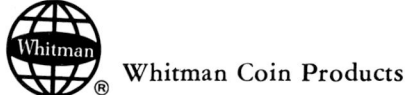 Whitman Coin Products

Copyright © 1977, 1963, 1959, 1953 by
WESTERN PUBLISHING COMPANY, INC.
RACINE, WISCONSIN 53404
All Rights Reserved

WHITMAN is a registered trademark of Western Publishing Company, Inc.
Library of Congress Catalog Card No.: 77-075030

9057   ISBN: 0-307-09057-4   Printed in U.S.A.

CONTENTS

Coinage Before the Time of the Empire	8
Roman Coin Denominations	14
Praenomen—Nomen—Cognomen	18
The Obverse Inscriptions	22
Names of Emperors as They Appear on Coins	28
Informal and Formal Names of Emperors	33
Reverse Figures (Deities and Personifications)	37
Reverse Inscriptions	51
Mint Marks	58
Chronological Sketches of Emperors, Etc.	60
Determining the Year a Coin Was Struck	101
Dates of the Tribunicia Potestas	120
Bibliography	125

Introduction to the Fourth Edition

Nearly twenty-five years ago I made certain statements in the introduction to the first edition of this book that are valid today. I emphasized that this was a handbook for beginners and that an understanding of the subject would come not only from a serious study of the coins themselves, but from familiarity with the principal works on Roman Imperial coins. These, I would suggest, are Cohen's "Description historique des monnais frapées sous l'Empire romain"; "The Roman Imperial Coinage," by Mattingly and Sydenham and "Coins of the Roman Empire in the British Museum," by Mattingly and by Carson.

Ancient coins have advanced considerably in price in the years since the last edition of this book was published in 1963, but it is still possible to purchase specimens at prices that surely must be considered bargains. Yet, regardless of price, how does one place a value on the experience of holding in one's hand a little fragment of the past? To me, there is a steadying influence in this: those who handled the coins many, many centuries ago sustained the same problems which affect us today. And they all are dust now, long forgotten.

I have been asked about counterfeits. The wise collector purchases his coins from reputable dealers of whom there are many in this country and abroad, all of whom will guarantee the authenticity of the items they sell. There is also available Sir George Hill's valuable work, "Becker the Counterfeiter." Also, sometime this year I hope, my own book on imitations and inventions of Roman coins will be in print. This work consumed nearly five years of my time including study of the coins themselves at the principal cabinets in this country and in Europe. Basically, this is an examination of the so-called Paduans; medals struck by Renaissance engravers.

Many people were kind enough to have helped me with this work and, once again, I thank them. I am, however, most grateful to my critics who, although I have wished some of them would have dealt a little kindlier with me(!), were interested enough to point out errors which enabled me, with each edition, to eliminate them. I hope few remain in this edition.

Finally, I have been criticized, perhaps with some justification, for not extending this book to include more about the coinage of the late Empire. Generally, these coins are among the least expensive to collect. However, the cost of printing and publishing today precludes such an extension, particularly when it is the publisher's intent to bring out books at a modest price.

Zander H. Klawans

Coinage Before the Time of the Empire

Before discussing the coins of the Roman Empire it is of interest to know a little about the background of these coins and about the development which led to their coming into existence.

One of the Latin words for money is PECUNIA, which originates from the shorter Latin word, PECUS, meaning CATTLE. It may not at once be recognized that there is a connection between cattle and money but a brief analysis will show a definite wedding of the two words. Cattle provide sustenance, in one form or another, for humankind. Something with such a universal appeal and of such vital necessity to almost all mankind has positive value. Thus, cattle had value in ancient times. With cattle a man could buy the other necessities of life and wealth could be measured by the number of heads of cattle a man possessed.

Obviously, such bulky material was an inadequate means of exchange. The problems of transporting hundreds of heads of cattle here and there was a great one and it became more intense when the world markets of those days started to blossom; trading in cattle became cumbersomely impossible. The logical answer was the creation of a means of exchange, universally recognized, but small in size. Coinage was the answer.

When Rome first began to flex her muscles and feel the surge of a newborn power she required, and obtained, this more flexible system. This first coinage was crude, shapeless, and heavy in an attempt to approximate the value of the coin with its actual weight. The first coinage, a cast coinage, was called AES RUDE (rude, or crude bronze. The Latin word for bronze is AES). These first coins probably were struck in the

5th century B.C. They have been found in various shapes, rectangular, flat, square, and in lumps.

Sometime during the third century B.C. a medium of exchange called AES SIGNATUM came into use. These large, cumbersome pieces carried the images of animals, such as birds and cattle upon them, and also inanimate objects, such as tridents and shields. It would seem to be a mistake to call such pieces "money" rather than to consider them as having been used as a means of exchange on the basis of weight.

There next came into existence the coinage which was to be forerunner of all coinage to come. It was called AES GRAVE (Heavy bronze) and while it was still a cast coin, it was circular in shape. Scholars differ as to the approximate date this coinage came into existence, but the year 300 B.C. or thereabouts should suffice. The AES GRAVE was cast in various denominations. We list them as the AS, the SEMIS, the TRIENS, the QUADRANS, the SEXTANS, and the UNCIA. Each of these coins could be distinguished from the other by the obverse (front) of the coin. The AS always had the head of the god Janus; the SEMIS pictured Jupiter; the TRIENS, Minerva; the QUADRANS, Hercules; the SEXTANS, Mercury; the UNCIA, Roma. The prow of a ship is found on the reverse of all these denominations, undoubetedly indicative of Rome's new found respect for the sea and her turning to the sea and to new lands.

Rome now had to accomplish two things; she had to create a coinage which would be recognized in the land she had conquered or in the land with which she was trading. Thus, it was necessary to emulate the coinage of these countries. Secondly, it was necessary to create a less cumbersome coinage, a coinage which could easily be transported both across the sea and in Italy itself. Both these problems were successfully resolved by the coinage of a silver piece long familiar to the Greeks (and the Romans did inherit from the Greeks) known as the DRACHMA and the coinage of copper coins as

[9

AS
Janus

SEMIS
Jupiter

TRIENS
Minerva

QUADRANS
Hercules

SEXTANS
Mercury

UNCIA
Roma

REVERSE TYPE
Prow of Ship

well. These coins were the first struck coins of Rome (about 269 B.C.).

Later, possibly about the beginning of the 2nd century B.C., the Romans issued coins which were peculiarly their own. These were the DENARIUS, the SESTERTIUS and the QUINARIUS. We find coins bearing these same names during the time of the empire, but with the exception of the denarius there is little resemblance between these early coins and the later ones. The year 187 B.C. had for some time been accepted as the beginning date of the denarius, but fairly recent excavations at Morgantina in Sicily suggest the period of the second Punic War (218-201 B.C.).

Throughout this transition cast coins were still in existence but they were constantly being lowered in weight essentially because of the inflation which accompanied and followed the Punic Wars, a series of three wars against the Carthaginians (264-241 B.C.; 218-201 B.C.; 149-146 B.C.). The end of these wars found Rome on the verge of bankruptcy, a result of which was that the coinage was in a constant state of flux. The weights of the coins were reduced and all the evils of a real inflation were in evidence. No man really knew what his money was worth. However, the final victory of Rome over Carthage in 146 B.C. led to a gradual but determined reorganization of the coinage and at this time all coinage was struck; there were no more cast coins. The denarius emerged as the common coin of the realm and it remained virtually unchanged until the time of the empire. Gold was also struck, but this was in the nature of an emergency and it did not, at this time, form a regular part of the Roman coinage.

It was not long before the coins started to take on a real interest in many ways. There was more of an effort to make them more pleasing from an artistic standpoint. The reverses, in particular, became media for a multitude of objects of a religious, political, historical, and architectural nature. Deities and personifications appeared in great numbers. The coinage had come into its own! There were variances of style and texture to the extent that later-day numismatists would be able to classify these coins both chronologically and geographically.

Roman Coin Denominations

In order to possess a reasonable knowledge of the coins of the Roman Empire it is necessary to know the names by which they are called and to be able to distinguish them from one another.

There were not a great many denominations struck during the period of the Empire and so the beginner should not have too much difficulty in naming them. Certain denominations, such as those struck in gold and some which appeared late in the history of the Empire are either quite rare or costly and, therefore, are infrequently seen by the greater majority of collectors. Others are extremely common and it is these coins which form the background of most collections. Probably the most common coins of the period of the Empire are the:

Denarius of Otho
(69 A.D.)

DENARIUS
DUPONDIUS
AS
SESTERTIUS
ANTONINIANUS
FOLLIS

The standard silver coin of the Empire was the DENARIUS. The DENARIUS was first issued about 187 B.C., or, as some scholars feel, during the 2nd Punic War, and remained in existence until about 296 A.D. During this period of years the coin was debased, mostly from the time of the Emperor Nero (54-68 A.D.) onward. At the beginning of the Emperor Caracalla's reign (211-217 A.D.) the DENARIUS was about 40% silver. It was at this time that the ANTONINIANUS appeared.

The ANTONINIANUS derived its name from the Emperor Caracalla (M. Aurelius Antoninus Caracalla, 211-217 A.D.) who first introduced it. This coin can be distinguished from the DENARIUS because the head of the subject on the ANTONINIANUS is radiate. This coin, too, had an auspicious beginning only to be debased to the status of a copper coin with a silver wash. Occasionally, it is possible to find a coin with the silver still present, but this is quite uncommon.

The coin was abolished at the time of Constantine the Great (308-337 A.D.).

Antoninianus of Tacitus (275-276 A.D.)

The DUPONDIUS was coined during the Imperial period until the time of Trajan Decius (249-251 A.D.) It was struck in brass and is quite often difficult to distinguish from the AS.

Dupondius of Augustus (29 B.C.-14 A.D.)

One means of determining the difference between the DUPONDIUS and the AS is by the color. The DUPONDIUS is

As of Domitian (81-96 A.D.)

a rather yellow color, while the AS is more reddish. Occasionally the AS was struck in orichalcum. In the later days of the empire it was the practice to strike the DUPONDIUS showing the head of the emperor radiate and the AS with a bare or laureated head.

The SESTERTIUS was the large coin of the empire and is known as large bronze or grand bronze. Upon the SESTERTIUS appear the most magnificent manifestations of the moneyer's art. The large size of the coin permitted the inclusion of the wonderful detail which was, of a necessity, lacking on the smaller coins. The SESTERTIUS was originally a silver coin of the Roman Republic, worth one quarter of a denarius.

Sestertius of Antoninus Pius (138-161 A.D.)

The Emperor Diocletian (284-304 A.D.) instituted the FOLLIS, which was a rather large coin with a silver wash.

Follis of Constantius (305-306 A.D.)

Other coins, not quite as common as those mentioned above were the:

CENTENIONALIS—A bronze coin which had its inception during the reign of Constantine (308-337 A.D.). It was bronze with a silver wash. After the time of Arcadius (395-408 A.D.) it sunk into obscurity.

QUADRANS—The fourth part of the AS. Struck in copper.

QUINARIUS—A silver coin about one-half the weight of the DENARIUS. It was issued only at intervals.

SEMIS—These coins were mostly of bronze with very little silver. The coin was issued from the time of the Republic on, and appeared in various sizes and types. It was also used for the Roman half aureus (The aureus was a gold coin). The term SEMISSIS was used to designate the SEMIS when used as a half of the aureus or solidus.

SOLIDUS—A gold coin issued by Constantine the Great (308-337 A.D.).

AUREUS—The best known of the Roman gold coins. Appeared at about the time of Julius Caesar (45-44 B.C.). The weight of this coin gradually declined until, at the time of Constantine (308-337 A.D.), it was abolished to be replaced by the solidus.

SILIQUA—A Roman silver coin, first issued by Constantine the Great (308-337 A.D.). It was equivalent to 1/24 solidus.

The Relationship of the Coins to Each Other

The small table which follows will help to distinguish the relationship of the principal coins to each other. The reader will also notice that the larger coins do not necessarily carry the larger value.

Collectors of ancient coins always seem to have been plagued with the question of what a particular coin would have purchased, in terms of the present. Perhaps an answer could be found for a *specific* period in Roman history, although this seems doubtful. We must remember that while a sestertius, for example, might have purchased a loaf of bread during a certain period of Roman history, that same sestertius could not have done so during another period. If we were to study our own monetary system, we would find the same to be true. During inflationary periods, our dollar is worth less than during times of fiscal stability: an automobile may cost three or four times as much as it did 20 or 25 years ago and this would apply to all commodities. The Romans were no different. They, too, went through periods of depression and prosperity . . . and prosperity with inflation.

Using the denarius as a base, the following relationships prevail:

COIN	NUMBER TO THE DENARIUS
SESTERTIUS	4
DUPONDIUS	8
AS	16
QUADRANS	64

[17

PRAENOMEN   NOMEN   COGNOMEN

Before taking up the discussion of the obverse (front) of the Roman coins it would be best first to mention the proper names and the way they are found upon the coins. If it is possible to remember two important facts the reading of the proper names upon the coins should not present a problem.

First: The Roman first name (praenomen) was always regularly abbreviated, not from choice but as a designation of Roman citizenship.

Second: The abbreviation "IMP" (Imperator) was regularly used, from the earliest times in the Empire, as a praenomen.

Perhaps the best, and simplest way to describe the terms NOMEN, PRAENOMEN, and COGNOMEN is to look to our own usage in present times. The Latin word NOMEN means "name." The prefix, PRAE, means "before." Thus, PRAENOMEN means "before name" or, the first name. COGNOMEN is the last name or surname. The Roman name was not a fixed or absolute form. It varied throughout the history of Rome. At the first a man was called by one name only. Gradually this was developed into a combination with the genitive case wherein it was then indicated that that person came under the authority of another. A daughter was under the authority of her father; a wife, under the authority of her husband; a slave was subservient to his master. And so we would see a name written in this manner; Marcus Marci f (Marcus, the son of Marcus). The single letter "f" designates filius, the Latin word for son. The single letter "f," in the case of a woman would indicate the Latin word filia, daughter.

Entering further upon the subject let us now be more specific and instead of saying that the praenomen, nomen, and cognomen are the first, middle and last names, respectively, we shall say that the praenomen was the given name, the individual name; the nomen is the name of the gens, or the clan, if you will, and the cognomen is the name of the family which is a part of that gens or clan. Thus: L. Cornelius Scipio; "L" is the abbreviation of the Latin name Lucius, and it is the praenomen, the given name. "Cornelius" is the nomen, the name of the gens or the clan to which this person's family belongs. "Scipio" is the family name. It is also the cognomen. The Scipio family is a part of the Cornelian gens.

Praenomen

The praenomen, as has been before mentioned, was the strictly personal name. It was conferred by the parents upon the child probably on the 9th day after birth, in the case of boys and the 8th day after birth in the case of girls. There has been some disagreement on this point because many inscriptions on tombstones have indicated that older boys and girls were nameless and the word "Pupio" appears on many of the stones in the absence of a praenomen. (Pupio, child.)

As stated before the praenomen was regularly abbreviated when used with the nomen and cognomen. This was not a matter of choice but an established custom indicating Roman citizenship. This is a very good point to remember when reading coins, for the praenomina invariably are abbreviated. The following list gives the more common praenomina with their abbreviations:

```
AULUS............A, AU, AUL (rare), O (very rare)
DECIMUS.........D, DEC (Rare and late)
CAIUS or GAIUS...C
GNAEUS..........CN, GN (Very rare)
LUCIUS...........L, LU (rare)
MARCUS..........M
PUBLIUS..........P, PUP (rare)
QUINTUS.........Q
SERVIUS.........SER
```

SERGIUS..........S (rare)
SEXTUS...........SEX, SX
SPURIUS..........S, SP
TIBERIUS.........TI
TITUS.............T
APPIUS...........AP, AP P (rare)
NUMERICUS......N
VIBIUS............V

The patrician families usually used the same praenomina for all members of their family . . . that is, the same group of praenomina. A list which might prove to be of some help follows, showing the better known families and the praenomina which they used:

AEMILII.....C, CN, L, MAM, M. Q, TI
CLAUDII.....AP, C, D, L, P. TI, Q
CORNELII...A, CN, L, M, P, SER, TI
FABII........C, K, M, N, Q
FURII.......AGRIPPA, C, L, M, SEX, SP
JULII........C, L, SEX
MANLII......A, CN, L, M.

Nomen

The nomen is the name which belonged to all members of the same family. At first this name was identified with a certain locality. Later, it was indicative of members of the same gens, or clan. The nomen usually ended in "ius," "aius," "eius," "eus." Thus, Aemilius, Cornelius, Furius, Manlius, Pompeius.

Cognomen

The cognomen was, at first, a personal name. Later it became a family name, the name of a family within a particular gens, or clan. Thus, of the gens Cornelius there were the Cethegi, Lentuli, and the Scipiones, to name a few.

Perhaps the clearest way to picture the entire subject of Latin names is to give a present day analogy. The analogy given is a rather "liberal" one, but it shall serve our purpose. Some people carry the maiden name of their mother as a second, or "middle" name. Thus, John Scott Pauley, as an example, would show his first name, John (praenomen), the family name of his mother, Scott (nomen), and the name of his own family, Pauley (cognomen). If this example is kept in mind it should be helpful in reading the coins.

The Obverse Inscriptions

There are many methods of collecting Roman coins. Some collections consist of the reverse types; others emphasize a particular reverse type such as the various coins bearing the images of Concordia (Harmony), or Fides (Faith), or of other personifications and deities. Undoubtedly, however, most collections are portrait collections, portraits of the emperors and their contemporaries upon the obverse (front) part of the coin. Perhaps the most interesting is that grouping in which the collector has specialized in the large bronze coins known as sestertii. The large size of this coin enabled the classical engravers to include an abundance of detail which was quite difficult to impress upon coins of smaller dimensions. Any collection, of course, is a matter of the personal taste of the particular collector, and a fine collection of portraits, regardless of the medium used, will make a most attractive display. New collectors experience their greatest difficulty in attempting to read the coins. This is quite interesting because many students of Latin are unable to read the inscriptions simply because of the profusion of abbreviations appearing upon them. Yet, many people who possess fine collections are not students of Latin, and need not be. By remembering certain commonly used abbreviations, a person of average intelligence can read many of the coins which he would come across, provided, of course, that the inscription is legible.

Essentially, the most confusing thing is the habit the Romans possessed of running the entire inscription together with no "break" between the words. A typical inscription appearing upon a sestertius of Nero is an excellent example. For the sake of clarity and simplicity the coin has been subdivided into its logical parts.

Thus, we find we have:

NERO CLAUD CAESAR AUG GER PM TR P IMP PP

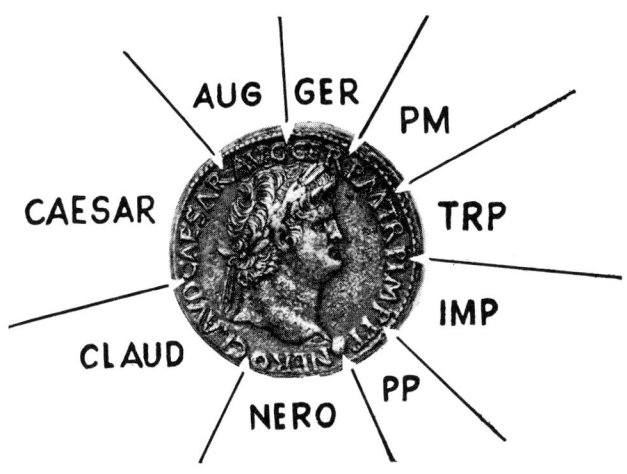

If the reader will remember the very few common abbreviations, abbreviations which appear time and time again on almost all the coins of the early empire, the inscription should present no difficulties.

Aug Augustus (or Augusta, if feminine). This was the most distinctive of all of the imperial titles. It was used by no one but the reigning emperor or members of his family. It appears with most frequent regularity on the coins.

PM
Pon M
Pon Max
Pontifex Max etc.

Another very common title of the emperor. Pontifex Maximus was the emperor's title as supreme head of the Roman religion (Literally, Head priest). The title was held by the emperor Augustus and all subsequent emperors.

TR P
Trib P
Trib Pot
Trib Potest
Tribun Potest, etc.

Tribunicia Potestate. The tribunician power. From earliest times, the tribunes were the representatives of the Roman people and, at various times, held tremendous power. Thus, the Tribunician power represents the emperor's position in that light, although more specifically, it showed him to be the supreme civil head of the state. The Tr P is quite commonly

[23

found with Roman numerals following it. This is an excellent tool to determine the year a particular coin was struck. (A chart is incorporated in this book for the purpose of determining such a date.)

COS COS is the abbreviation for consul. The consul was one of the two chief magistrates of the Roman state. The emperor himself quite frequently was one of the consuls: when he was not, he usually appointed the person to serve in his place. The COS, as with the TR P, is often followed by Roman numerals. Inasmuch as a consulship lasted for but a year, it is here also possible to determine the date a particular coin was struck by reference to the chart incorporated in this book.

PP PATER PATRIAE. Father of his country. This inscription appears on many of the coins and was originally a title bestowed upon the emperor by the senate. Some emperors refused the title.

IMP IMPERATOR. Emperor, generally, although the title was bestowed upon victorious generals in the field during the Republican period and the period of the very early empire. From the time of the emperor Tiberius onward, it was a title used by no one other than the emperor himself.

Now, in looking once more at the above inscription of Nero, we are able to understand the logical breakdown and the complete meaning of the inscription.

1. Nero...His name.

2. Claud...Claudius. The name of the gens to which his family belonged. His nomen.

3. Caesar...The inherited name of the Julian family and adopted by the Claudian family. Also adopted by subsequent emperors, and later used by heirs to the throne.

4. Augustus...The most distinctive title of the emperor.

24]

5. Ger...Germanicus. A hereditary title, as well as a title of honor.

6. PM...Pontifex Maximus. The highest priest. The head of the Roman religion.

7. TR P...Tribunicia Potestate. The tribunician power. The civil head of state.

8. IMP...Imperator. This use of Imperator is as a title of acclamation such as for victories in the field of the emperor or his subordinates.

9. PP...Pater Patriae. Father of his country.

Here is another coin, a sestertius of the Emperor Titus. Again, for the sake of convenience, we have subdivided the title.

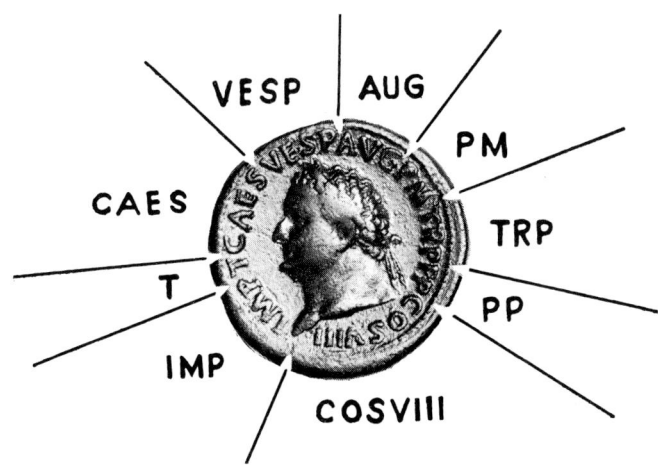

The complete inscription on the coin
IMP T CAES VESP AUG PM TRP PP COS VIII

Let us again analyze the inscription.

1. IMP...Imperator, Emperor.

2. T...Titus, his name, or praenomen.

3. Caes...Caesar.

[25

4. Vesp...Vespasian. The cognomen of the emperor Titus. It was a common practice for an emperor to take as a part of his name the name of his predecessor, particularly if that predecessor had adopted him as his legal heir or if he was the natural heir, as in the case of Titus.

5. Aug...Augustus.

6. PM...Pontifex Maximus.

7. TR P...Tribunicia Potestate.

8. PP...Pater Patriae. Father of his country.

9. COS VIII...In his eighth consulship. This coin was struck during the eighth consulship of Titus. Checking with the chart in this book it is indicated that the eighth consulship of Titus occurred in the year 80 AD. Thus, the coin pictured here was struck in that year.

As a final example we shall take a coin, an AS, of Domitian, Here again the coin has been struck off into its subdivisions.

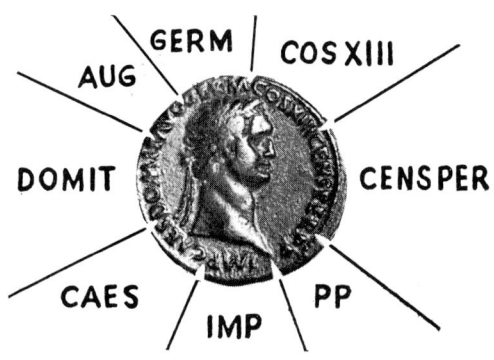

The complete inscription
IMP CAES DOMIT AUG GERM COS XIII CENS PER PP

1. IMP...Imperator. Emperor. Here, however, there is a little different use of the title, for it is used as a praenomen, or a given name.

2. CAES...Caesar.

3. DOMIT...Domitian. His name.

4. AUG...Augustus.

5. GERM...Germanicus.

6. COS XIII...In his 13th consulship. Using the chart in this book, we see that the 13th consulship of Domitian occurred in the year 87 AD. 87 AD., then, was the year in which this coin was struck.

7. CENS PER...Censor Perpetuus. The censor was a chief magistrate of the Roman state. The title was quite frequently held by the emperor and was granted for his lifetime. (Thus, the "Perpetuus.")

8. PP...Pater Patriae. Father of his country.

An Alphabetical Check List of the Names of the Emperors as They Frequently Appear on the Coins

This section offers, in alphabetical sequence, the names of the emperors as they appear upon the coins with considerable frequency. The second column presents the names of the emperors as they are commonly known. For example, a coin with the name C CAESAR upon it can be located in the first column. Directly opposite, in the second column, we find that emperor's common name, CALIGULA.

It should be noted that the alphabetical column lists the names exactly as they would appear upon the coin and, as a result, are abbreviated either in part or in whole. For the inquisitive reader, it might be of interest to note the grammatical case differences in some of the names. Most of the names are in the nominative case and yet we find, as in the case of the emperor Trajan, an ending which would not be in the nominative case. TRAIANUS is the nominative ending, but we find the inscription to read, TRAIANO. This is an example of the dative case. Thus, instead of reading, THE EMPEROR TRAJAN AUGUSTUS, etc., as we would expect, it reads, *TO* . . . THE EMPEROR TRAJAN AUGUSTUS, etc.

Many times it is difficult to identify the emperor by name alone for some emperors possessed identical names. The photographs of the emperors in the section of this book which includes the biographies should be of some assistance. Gordianus I and Gordianus II, father and son, had identical names, yet the coins reveal that the elder Gordian had hair well down upon his forehead while the younger Gordian is shown with a bald forehead. Most of the coins of Marcus Aurelius show portraits which are very similar and this should preclude any confusion with other emperors who bore similar titles. Reference to the plates contained in some of the fine volumes which may be found upon the shelves of the larger libraries will supply invaluable assistance in identification. A list of some of the more important works appears in the bibliography at the end of this book.

| **Name as It Frequently Appears on the Coins** | **Common Name** |

A

A Vitellius Germanicus	*Vitellius*
Ant Pius Aug	*Caracalla*
Antoninus Aug Pius	*Antoninus Pius*
Antoninus Pius Fel	*Elagabalus*

B

| Brittanicus | *Brittanicus* |
| Brut Imp | *Brutus* |

C

C Caesar	*Caligula*
C Caesar Aug	*Augustus*
C Iul Verus Maximus	*Maximus*
C M Aur Marius	*Marius*
C Valens Hostil Mes Quintus	*Hostilian*
Caesar	*Julius Caesar*
Caesar Dict	*Julius Caesar*
Constantinus Max Aug	*Constantine the Great*

D

D Clod Sept	*Clodius Albinus*
D N Ancius Olybrius	*Olybrius*
D N Constantius	*Constantius II*
D N Decentius	*Decentius*
D N Gratianus	*Gratian*
D N Honorius	*Honorius*
D N Iulius Maioranus	*Majorian*
D N Iovianus	*Jovian*
D N Mag Maximus	*Magnus Maximus*
D N Martininianus	*Martinian*
D N Theodosius	*Theodosius I (The Great)*
D N Valentinianus	*Valentinian I*

**Name as It Frequently
Appears on the Coins**   **Common Name**

F

Fl Cl Constantinus Iun............*Constantine II*
Fl Cl Iulianus....................*Julian II*
Fl Cl Hanniballiano Regi..........*Hanniballianus*
Fl Iul Constans..................*Constans*
Fl Iul Constantius...............*Constantius II*
Fl Iul Delmatius.................*Delmatius*
Fl Nep Constantinus..............*Neoptian*
Fl Val Constantius...............*Constantius I (Chlorus)*
Fl Val Severus...................*Severus II*

G

Germanicus Caesar................*Germanicus*
Gal Val Maximianus...............*Galerius*
Gal Val Maximinus................*Maximinus II (Gaza)*

H

Hadrianus Aug....................*Hadrian*

I

Imp T Ael Caes Hadrianus Antoninus *Antoninus Pius*
Imp Caes Aemilianus..............*Aemilian*
Imp D Cl Sep Alb.................*Clodius Albinus*
Imp Sev Alexander................*Severus Alexander*
Imp Antoninus....................*Elagabalus*
Imp Caes M Aur Anton.............*Caracalla*
Imp Caes M Aurel Antoninus.......*Marcus Aurelius*
Imp C L Dom Aurelianus...........*Aurelian*
Imp C M Aur Sev Alexander........*Severus Alexander*
Imp C D Cael Balbinus............*Balbinus*
Imp C Carausius..................*Carausius*
Imp C M Aur Carus................*Carus*
Imp C Claudius...................*Claudius II*
Imp Caes D Cl Sep Alb............*Clodius Albinus*
Imp Constantinus.................*Constantine the Great*

Name as It Frequently Appears on the Coins	Common Name
Imp Caes M Did Sever Iulian	Didius Julianus
Imp C Diocletianus	Diocletian
Imp Caes Domit	Domitian
Imp Cl Domitius Domitianus	Domitius Domitianus
Imp C M An Florianus	Florianus
Imp Ser Galba Aug	Galba
Imp C D Lic Gallienus	Gallienus
Imp Caes P Sept Geta	Geta
Imp Caes M Ant Gordianus	Gordian I and II
Imp Gordianus Pius	Gordianus Pius (III)
Imp C Laelianus	Laelianus
Imp C Val Licin Licinius	Licinius I
Imp C Ful Macrianus	Macrianus II
Imp C M Opel Macrinus	Macrinus
Imp Caes Magnentius	Magnentius
Imp C Maxentius	Maxentius
Imp C M A Maximianus	Maximianus I (Hercules)
Imp Maximinus Pius Aug	Maximinus I
Imp Nero Caes	Nero
Imp Nerva Caes	Nerva
Imp M Otho Caes	Otho
Imp Ti Cl Mar Pacatian	Pacatian
Imp Caes P Helv Pertinax	Pertinax
Imp Caes C Pescennius Niger	Pescennius Niger
Imp Philippus Aug	Philip I
Imp M Iul Philippus	Philip I
Imp C Postumus	Postumus
Imp C Probus	Probus
Imp Caes Pupien	Pupienus
Imp C M Clod Pupienus	Pupienus
Imp C Ful Quietus	Quietus
Imp C P Q Regalianus	Regalianus
Imp C M Aur Sev Alexander	Severus Alexander
Imp Sev Alexander	Severus Alexander
Imp C M Cl Tacitus	Tacitus
Imp C Tetricus	Tetricus I

Name as It Frequently Appears on the Coins	Common Name
Imp Traiano Aug	*Trajan*
Imp Caes Nervae Traiano	*Trajan*
Imp Traianus Decius	*Trajan Decius*
Imp C C Trebonianus Gallus	*Trebonianus Gallus*
Imp Caes L Aurel Verus	*Lucius Verus*
Imp Caes Vesp	*Vespasian*
Imp T Caes Vesp	*Titus*
Imp C Piav Victorinus	*Victorinus*
Imp Cae C Vib Volusiano	*Volusian*

L

L Aelius Caesar	*Aelius*
L Aurel Commodus	*Commodus*
L Iul Aur Sulp Ura Antoninus	*Uranius Antoninus*
L Sept Sev	*Septimius Severus*
L Septimius Geta Caes	*Geta*
Licinius Iun	*Licinius II*

M

M Agrippa	*Agrippa*
M Antoni	*Marc Anthony*
M Aur Anton Caes	*Caracalla*
M Aur Carinus	*Carinus*
M Aur Numerianus	*Numerian*
M Commodus Antoninus	*Commodus*
M Lepidus	*Lepidus*
M Opel Antoninus Diadumenianus	*Diadumenian*
Mag Decentius	*Decentius*
Magnus Pius	*Pompey the Great*
Maximinus Pius Aug Germanicus	*Maximinus I*

N

Nero Caes Aug	*Nero*
Nero Claudius Caesar	*Nero*
Nero Claudius Drusus	*Nero Claudius Drusus*

Name as It Frequently Appears on the Coins	Common Name
P	
P Sept Geta Caes	*Geta*
Q	
Q Her Etr Mes Decius	*Herennius Etruscus*
S	
Ser Galba Imp Caes	*Galba*
T	
T Caes Imp	*Titus*
Ti Caes Augustus	*Tiberius*
Ti Claud Caes	*Claudius*

The Informal and Formal Names of the Emperors

As an additional aid, and in order to provide additional information, the following two columns present, first, the informal or common names of the emperors and some of their contemporaries and, in the second column, their formal names.

Common Name   Full Name

Aelius...Lucius Aelius Verus Caesar
Aemilian...Marcus Aemilius Aemilianus
Agrippa...Marcus Vipsania Agrippa
Antoninus Pius...Titus Aelius Hadrianus Antoninus
Augustus...Caius Iulius Caesar Octavianus
Aurelian...Lucius Domitius Aurelianus

Balbinus...Decimus Caelius Balbinus
Brutus...Marcus Iunius Brutus
Brittanicus...Tiberius Claudius Brittanicus

Caligula...Caius Caesar
Caracalla...Marcus Aurelius Antoninus
Carausius...Marcus Aurelius Mausaeus Carausius

Common Name   Full Name
Carus...Marcus Aurelius Carus
Claudius...Tiberius Claudius Drusus
Claudius II...Marcus Aurelius Claudius
Clodius Albinus...Decimus Clodius Ceionius Septimius Albinus
Constans...Flavius Iulius Constans
Constantine the Great...Flavius Valerius Constantinus
Constantine II...Flavius Claudius Iulius Constantinus
Constantius I (Chlorus)...Flavius Valerius Constantius
Constantius II...Flavius Iulius Constantius

Decentius...Magnus Decentius
Delmatius...Flavius Iulius Delmatius
Diadumenian...Marcus Opelius Antoninus Diadumenianus
Didius Julianus...Marcus Didius Salvius Iulianus
Diocletian...Caius Valerius Diocletianus
Domitian...Titus Flavius Domitianus
Domitius Domitianus...Lucius Domitius Domitianus

Elagabalus...Marcus Aurelius Antoninus

Florian...Marcus Annius Florianus

Galba...Servius Sulpicius Galba
Galerius...Galerius Valerius Maximianus
Gallienus...Publius Licinius Valerianus Egnatis Gallienus
Germanicus...Germanicus
Geta...Lucius (or Publius) Septimius Geta
Gordian I and III (Pius)...Marcus Antonius Gordianus
Gordian II...Marcus Antonianus Gordianus
Gratian...Flavius Gratianus

Hadrian...Publius Aelius Hadrianus
Hanniballianus...Flavius Claudius Hanniballianus
Herennius Etruscus...Quintus Herrenius Etruscus Messius Decimus
Honorius...Flavius Honorius
Hostilian...Caius Valens Hostilianus Messius Quintus

Jovian...Flavius Claudius Iovianus

Common Name   Full Name

Julius Caesar...Caius Iulius Caesar
Julian I...Marcus Aurelius Iulianus
Julian II...Flavius Claudius Iulianus

Laelianus...Ulpius Cornelius Laelianus
Lepidus...Marcus Aemilius Lepidus
Licinius I...Publius Flavius Galerius Valerius Licianus Licinius
Licinius II...Flavius Valerius Licinianus Licinius

Macrianus I...Marcus Fulvius Macrianus
Macrianus II...Titus Fulvius Iulius Macrianus
Macrinus...Marcus Opelius Severus Macrinus
Magnentius...Flavius Magnus Magnentius
Magnus Maximus...Magnus Clemens Maximus
Majorian...Iulianus Maiorianus
Marc Anthony...Marcus Antonius
Marcus Aurelius...Marcus Aelius Aurelius Verus
Marius...Caius Marcus Aurelius Marius
Martinian...Marcus Martinianus
Maxentius...Marcus Aurelius Valerius Maxentius
Maximianus I (Herculius)...Marcus Aurelius Valerius Maximianus
Maximinus I...Caius Iulius Verus Maximinus
Maximinus II (Daza)...Galerius Valerius Maximinus

Nepotian...Flavius Popilius Nepotianus Constantinus
Nero...Nero Claudius Caesar Drusus Brittanicus
Nero Claudius Drusus...Nero Claudius Drusus
Nerva...Marcus Cocceius Nerva
Numerian...Marcus Aurelius Numerianus

Olybrius...Ancius Olybrius
Otho...Marcus Salvius Otho

Pacatian...Tiberius Claudius Mar Pacatian
Pertinax...Publius Helvius Pertinax
Pescennius Niger...Caius Pescennius Niger
Philip I...Marcus Iulius Philippus

[35

Common Name   Full Name

Pompey the Great...Cnaeus Pompeius Magnus
Postumus...Marcus Cassianus Latinus Postumus
Probus...Marcus Aurelius Probus
Pupienus...Marcus Clodius Pupienus Maximus

Quietus...Fulvius Julius Quietus

Regalianus...Publius Caius Regalianus

Saturninus...Sextus Iulius Saturninus
Septimius Severus...Lucius Septimius Severus
Severus Alexander...Marcus Aurelius Severus Alexander
Severus II...Flavius Valerius Severus
Sextus Pompey...Sextus Pompeius Magnus

Tacitus...Marcus Claudius Tacitus
Tetricus I...Caius Pius Esuvius Tetricus
Theodosius I (The Great)...Flavius Theodosius
Tiberius...Tiberius Claudius Nero
Titus...Titus Flavius Sabinus Vespasianus
Trajan...Marcus Ulpius Traianus
Trajan Decius...Caius Messius Quintus Traianus Decius
Trebonianus Gallus...Caius Vibius Trebonianus Gallus
Uranius Antoninus...Lucius Iulius Aurelius Sulpicius Uranius Antoninus

Valentinian I...Flavius Valentinianus
Vespasian...Titus Flavius Sabinus Vespasianus
Victorinus...Marcus Piavvonius Victorinus
Vitellius...Aulus Vitellius
Volusian...Caius Vibius Volusianus Trebonianus Gallus

The Reverse Figures on Roman Coins
(Deities and Personifications)

The variety of figures on the reverse of the coins is a subject of more than passing interest. The types are numerous and a partial list is included here. Many of the coins picture a deity or a personification. A personification is the personalizing of a place or of a thing. Concordia, as an example is the personalizing of a thing, concord or harmony; Fortuna is the personification of fortune, and so on. Most frequently, a figure may be identified by carefully observing its dress, or the objects held by the figure, or the position of the figure itself. For example, it will be noted that Spes, the personification of "hope," is usually found walking, holding a flower, and slightly lifting her skirt. A coin with this personification upon it would need no spelled-out description, for no other figure is represented in a similar manner. Hercules, a deity, appears as a powerful man, wearing a lion skin, and with a club in his hand. As such, he should easily be recognizable.

The reader should remember that all inscriptions appearing on the reverses do not necessarily refer to, or identify, the figure.

Deities

Aesculapius

AESCULAPIUS—The god of Medicine and of healing. He is shown holding a staff about which a serpent twines. (The insignia of the medical and dental corps of the United States Army.) He is sometimes accompanied by a small figure, Telesphorus, his attendant.

Apollo

APOLLO—The Sun god and god of Music and the Arts. He usually has the title Conservator, or Palatinus (Protector of the imperial residence on the Palatine) or Monetae (deity of the mint). He is usually holding a lyre.

Ceres

CERES—The goddess of Agriculture. Usually holding ears of corn, and frequently a torch.

Cybele

CYBELE—The mother of the gods. Usually wears a crown and is in a car drawn by lions or sits on a throne between lions.

DIANA—The Moon-goddess. Sometimes has a crescent of the moon above her head, or bow and arrows, accompanied by hounds or deer. Occasionally given the title of torch bearer (Lucifera) and holds a torch. Other titles are Conservatrix, Ephesia, and Victrix.

Diana

HERCULES—Representing Strength. Recognizable by his excellent physique and the club and lion skin.

Hercules

JANUS—A double-headed deity infrequently appearing on imperatorial coins. He was the god of the past and future (looking both ways).

Janus

JUPITER—Also Jove or Optimus Maximus (the Best and Highest or Greatest). Appears nude or semi-nude, with a full beard. Holds a thunderbolt in his right hand and a scepter in his left. He was the Father of the gods. The titles are different on the coins. On some he is called Conservator (the Conservator of the emperor or of the state), or Tonans (the thunderer), or Stator (the stayer of armies about to flee).

Jupiter

[39

Juno

JUNO—The wife of Jupiter. She holds a patera (a small dish used in Roman days for drinking or for the pouring of libations) and a scepter. Many times she is accompanied by a peacock. . . . Some of her titles are Regina (Queen), Lucina (as deity of childbirth), Conservatrix and Victrix.

LIBER—Bacchus. Liber is his Italian name. Usually holds a wine cup and a staff surmounted by a pine cone or a bunch of grapes (thyrsus) and accompanied by a panther.

Mars

MARS—The god of War. Shown, usually, with shield and spear, and is often nude with the exception of a helmet. Also, sometimes shown with a trophy instead of a shield. Some of his titles are Propugnator (fighter . . . for Rome), or Ultor (the Avenger). With the title Pacifer (Pacifyer) he bears the olive branch representing peace.

MERCURY—The Messenger of the gods. Usually wears a winged cap (petasus) and carries a purse and caduceus. Some of his titles are Pacifer and Conservator.

Mercury

MINERVA—Goddess of Wisdom. Patroness of the Arts. Also the light of men in war. She usually wears a shield and spear, and a helmet. Some of her titles are Pacifera and Victrix.

Minerva

NEPTUNE—God of the Sea. Usually holds a trident and a dolphin. The prow of a galley is sometimes included and many coin-types show him with his foot upon the prow.

Neptune

Roma

ROMA—The goddess of Rome. Usually helmeted and in armor. Holds a small figure of Victory at times, or a wreath, or a parazonium (a small sword or dagger).

Sol

SOL—The Sun-god. Usually nude with a radiate head, holding a whip or a globe. Sometimes he is shown in a chariot or with the horses of the sun included. His titles include Comes, Invictus, or, less frequently, Oriens (the rising, or eastern sun).

Venus

VENUS—The goddess of Love. Usually completely clothed or almost so. Some of her equipment includes an apple, or the helmet of Mars and a scepter. Sometimes accompanied by Cupid. Her titles include, Coelestis(Heavenly), Felix(Happy), Genetrix and Victrix.

Vesta

VESTA—Goddess of "family life." Shown as a matron holding a patera and scepter. Her titles include Sancta (Holy) and Mater (Mother). Consecratio sometimes appears as on this coin.

VULCAN—God of Fire and Iron. The Iron-Monger of the gods. Usually shown with the tools of the blacksmith's trade.

THE THREE GRACES — Euphrosyne, Aglaia, and Thalia. Lesser deities who presided over the banquet, the dance, and all social enjoyments and elegant arts. The three appear together.

The Three Graces

Personifications

Abundantia

ABUNDANTIA — Abundance, plenty. Holds ears of corn and cornucopiae (Horn of Plenty).

Aequitas

AEQUITAS—Fair dealing, equity. Holds scales and cornucopiae.

Aeternitas

AETERNITAS—Eternity, stability. Holds torch, globe or scepter, or the heads of the sun and the moon.

Annona

ANNONA—Corn harvest. Holds ears of corn and cornucopiae and is usually shown with the prow of a galley symbolizing the necessity of having corn shipped into Rome for its sustenance.

BONUS EVENTUS—Good luck, good fortune. A masculine personification. Holds patera over altar, and cornucopiae.

CLEMENTIA—Mercy, clemency. Holds branch and scepter, and sometimes leans upon a column.

Clementia

CONCORDIA—Harmony, concord. Holds scepter, patera or cornucopiae.

Concordia

FELICITAS—Happiness, prosperity. Holds cornucopiae and caduceus.

FIDES—Good faith, confidence. Holds patera and cornucopiae, or ears of corn and basket of fruit. As Fides Militum, holds two standards or other evidence of a military nature.

Felicitas

Fides

Fortuna

FORTUNA—Fortune. Holds rudder and cornucopiae. At times shown resting on globe. May also hold olive branch or patera.

Hilaritas

HILARITAS — Rejoicing, mirth. Holds cornucopiae and long palm. Sometimes two small children are shown and frequently one child.

Honos

HONOS—Honor. A masculine personification. Holds olive branch or scepter, and cornucopiae.

Indulgentia

INDULGENTIA—Indulgence, mercy. Holds patera and scepter.

JUSTITIA—Justice. Holds olive branch, or patera, and scepter. Infrequently she is seen holding scales.

Justitia

LAETITIA—Joy. Holds wreath and scepter, or occasionally a rudder on a globe in place of the scepter. She may rest her hand on an anchor.

Laetitia

LIBERALITAS—Liberality. Holds tablet (tessera) and cornucopiae.

Liberalitas

LIBERTAS—Liberty, freedom. Holds a pointed cap of liberty (pileus) and scepter.

Libertas

Moneta

MONETA—Money, mint. Holds scales and cornucopiae. Sometimes three figures appear, as pictured.

PATIENTIA—Patience, endurance. Holds scepter.

Pax

PAX—Peace. Holds olive branch and scepter, or cornucopiae.

Pietas

PIETAS—Piety, dutifulness. Quite frequently veiled. Holds patera and scepter. Sometimes is shown sacrificing at the altar.

PROVIDENTIA—Providence. Holds baton and scepter. Occasionally a globe appears at her feet.

Providentia

PUDICITIA—Chastity, modesty. Usually veiled holding scepter.

Pudicitia

SALUS—Health, welfare, safety. Holds patera from which she feeds a serpent coiled around an altar. Sometimes she is found holding the serpent in her arms and feeding it.

Salus

SECURITAS—Security, confidence. Holds scepter or patera.

Securitas

Spes

SPES—Hope. Holds flower. Is usually walking, slightly lifting her skirt.

Uberitas

UBERITAS—Fertility. Holds cornucopiae.

Victoria

VICTORIA—Victory, winged. Holds wreath and palm. May be bearing a shield or may be writing upon a shield or erecting a trophy. (The process of erecting a trophy was an ancient one and symbolized victory over the enemy in the field.)

Virtus

VIRTUS—A masculine personification for courage. Usually shown in complete armor, holding Victory and a spear, or a spear and a shield.

The Reverse Inscriptions on Roman Coins

The list of inscriptions included here is presented for the purpose of giving the reader a small cross section of the manifold varieties in existence. A complete list may be found in H. Cohen's *Description historique des monnais frappées sous l'Empire romain*. Quite frequently the value of a particular coin is determined by the reverse, for some reverses are much rarer than others.

Many of the coins are without inscriptions of any kind with the exception of the letters SC (on coins of the early empire) and figures representing deities or personifications. The letters SC, mean Senatus Consulto, by decree of the senate. The senate had under its control the minting of all coins other than those struck in gold. Practically speaking, this was merely pap thrown to the senate by the emperor, for he was supreme in every sense of the word, and remained so until the armies realized, only too quickly, that the elevation of an emperor was completely within their hands. Thus, S C, is a symbol, true, but a symbol which should not be taken too literally despite its universal use upon the coins.

The various combinations of inscriptions are exceedingly numerous. By "combination" it is meant the various adjectives which are used to describe the many different personalities. In the instance of Mars, we find:

> Mars Victor...........Mars the Victor
> Marti Conservatori.....(to) Mars the Conservator
> Marti Pacifer..........(to) Mars the Pacifyer
> Marti Propugnatori.....(to) Mars the Defender
> Mars Ultor............Mars the Avenger

And so on. These same adjectives are used to describe other Deities or personifications. Thus, for Jupiter we find, to name a few:

[51

Iovi Conservatori..... (to) Jupiter the Conservator
Iovi Statori.......... (to) Jupiter the Stabilizer or Provider
Iovi Propugnatori.... (to) Jupiter the Defender

In the later empire certain symbols became quite common. Among these are the abbreviated forms, singular and plural, of the words Dominus Noster (Our Lord, but in the liberal sense meaning our lord and ruler, of the Roman people). The symbol D N, therefore, means Dominus Noster, in one grammatical case or another. D D N N is the plural for D N and indicates two rulers or more. N N would be the plural for the word "our."

Thus,
>
> Victoria Aeterna Augg NN
> Eternal Victory of OUR emperors

The same interesting method of describing pluralities would apply in the case of the abbreviation, AUG, or CAES. Two rulers would be indicated by adding another "g" to the end of AUG. This would then show on the coin as AUGG. The same is true for the designation of Caesar. Two Caesars would be shown as CAESS. It was an excellent means of conserving space on the coin.

The inscriptions which follow are exactly as they appear on certain coins. This means that all or part of the inscription is abbreviated. It will be noted that many words which appear to the eye to be the same possess different endings. This is due to the exact use of the word within the inscription itself.

The endings are changed because of a change of grammatical case. And so Rome, in Latin, may appear as Romanorum, the genitive (possessive) case, or as Roma, the nominative case, depending upon its use. Venus, is the nominative case while Veneris, denotes the genitive (possessive) case. Keeping these examples in mind should prevent a considerable amount of confusion.

Finally, many of the inscriptions we are accustomed to observe on the obverse of the coin appear upon the reverse of quite a few coins. We find TR P, COS, PM, PP and others appearing as part of reverse inscriptions. In some instances the above are carried over from the obverse in order to complete the inscription.

The INSCRIPTIONS are printed in *Italic Type*.
Their LIBERAL MEANINGS are printed in Regular Type.

Inscription   **Liberal Meaning**

Advent Aug (or Augg)...Arrival of the emperor, or emperors.
Adventui Aug Felicissimo....Refers to the felicitations of the Roman people upon the return of the emperor.
Aeternae memoriae...(to) Eternal remembrance.
Apolloni sancto...(to) Holy Apollo.
Beata tranquillitas...Blessed Peace (of the state).
Bono Genio Pii Imperatoris...(to) the good Genius of the emperor.
Bonus Eventus...Good events, or happenings.
Cereri Frugif...(to) The fruit-bearing Ceres.
Claritas Reipub...Brightness of the Republic.
Clementia Temp...Clemency of the emperor (at the time).
Colonia Bostra...Colony of Bostra (Arabia).
Concord Aequit...Concord of Equity.
Concordia Augg...Concord of the emperors.
Concord Mili or Concordia Militum...Military concord.
Conserv Urb Suae...Conserver of the city (Rome).
Comiti Augg NN...Retinue of the emperors.
Dacia...A country.
Deo Vulcano...(to) The god Vulcan.
Diana Lucifera...Diana the bringer of light.
Dis Genitalibus...For having children.
D N Licini Augusti...(of) our lord Licinius, emperor.
Dominor Nostror Caess...Caesars, our lords.
Erculi Victori...To Hercules the Victor.
E X S.C. Ob Cives Servatos...A decree of the senate bestowed for having saved the lives of citizens.
Fecund Augustae...Fertility of the Empress.

Inscription	Liberal Meaning

Fel Temp Reparatio...Restoration of the happy times.
Felicitas Augg NN...Happiness of our emperors.
Felicitas Reipublicae...Happiness of the Republic.
Felix Advent Augg NN...Happy arrival of both our emperors.
Fides Exerc, or *Fides Exercitum*...Fidelity of the soldiers, or of the army.
Fides Mutua Augg...Mutual faith of the emperors.
Fort Red, or *Fortuna Redux*...Fortunate return of our emperor.
Fortunae Reduci Augg NN...(to) the fortunate return of our emperors.
Genio Antiocheni...Genius (Guardian) of Antioch.
Genio Augg et Caesarum NN...(to) the genius of the emperors and our Caesars.
Genio Augusti, Genio Imperatoris...(to) the genius of the emperor (or emperors).
Genio Pop Rom...(to) the genius of the Roman people.
Genius Senatus...Genius of the senate.
Germania...A country, province.
Gloria Novi Saeculi...The glory of the new age.
Gloria Romanorum...The glory of Rome. (Of the Romans.)
Hilaritas Augg...Mirth, or joy, of our emperors.
Hoc Signo Victor Eris...By this sign shalt thou be the victor (or, shalt thou conquer).
Honos...Honor.
Honos et *Virtus*...Honor and virtue.
Indulgentia Augg In Carth...Indulgence of the emperors to Carthage.
Iovi Conservatori Augg NN...(to) Jupiter, conservator of our emperors.
Iov Exsup, etc...Jove (Jupiter) who excels in all things.
Iovi Propugnatori...(to) Jupiter the defender.
Iovi Statori...(to) Jupiter the stabilizer.
Iovi Vot Susc Pro Sal Caes Aug SPQR...Vows to Jupiter by the senate and the Roman people for the restoration of the health of the emperor.
Iul...Julius, or Julia.
Iun...Junior.

Inscription   **Liberal Meaning**

Iuno Felix...Happy Juno.
Iuno Lucina...Goddess of light.
Iuno Regina...Juno the Queen.
Iunoni Martiali...(to) the war-like Juno.
Iuppitor Custos...Jupiter the custodian.
Iustitia...Justice.
Iuventus Augustus...The young Augustus.
Isis Faria...Isis, protectress of the Island of Pharos.
Laetit Fundata, Laetitia Fund...Well founded rejoicing.
Leg I, Leg II, Leg III, etc...The numbers of the legions.
Lib Aug, etc...Liberality of the emperor.
Mag Pius...Great and pious.
Mars Ultor...Mars, the avenger.
Mars Victor...Mars, the victor.
Mart Pac, Marti Pacif, or Pacifero...Mars, the pacifier.
Martia Conservatori...(to) Mars, the conserver.
Marti Propugt...(to) Mars, the defender.
Mauretania...A province.
Miliarum Saeculum...Commencement of the new era, or age.
Miner Fautr...Minerva who gives favors.
Moneta Aug...Money of the emperor.
Munificentia Aug...Munificence of the emperor.
N.F....Nobilissima Femina (Most noble woman).
Oriens Aug...Rising sun (of the emperor).
Pacator Orbis...Pacifier of the earth.
Pace Pr Ubiq Parta Ianum Clusit...Refers to the portal of Janus being closed, indicating peace.
Paci Augustae...To the peace of the emperor.
Par, Ar, Ad, etc...Parthia, Arabia, Adiabenius (conquered nations).
Pax Fundata Cum Persis...Firm peace with the Persians.
Pietas Mutua Aug...The mutual piety of the two Augusti.
Pietas Romana...Roman piety.
Popul Iussu...By order of the Roman people.
Primi Decennales...(of the) First period of ten years.

[55

| Inscription | Liberal Meaning |

Profectio Aug...The emperor setting out for a visit or expedition.

Prov Deor, Provid Deor, Providentia Deorum...Providence of the gods.

Providentiae Caess...Foresight of the Caesars.

Rector Orbis...Master of the world.

Regi Artis...(To the) King of the Arts.

Relig Aug...Religion of the emperor.

Reliqua Vetera H S Novies Mill Abolita..Refers to the liberality of the emperor (Hadrian) in remitting debts.

Reparatio Reipub...Restoration of the Republic.

Restitutor Africae...Restitutor, or ruler of Africa.

Restitutor Orbis...Restitutor, or ruler of the world.

Restitutor Urbis...Restitutor, or ruler of the city.

Sac Mon Urb Augg et Caes NN or Sacra Monet Augg et Caes Nostr...Sacred money of Rome, our emperors and our Caesars.

Saec Fel...Happy Age.

Saeculi (or Seculi) Felicitas...Happy Age (also, refers to the secular games).

Saeculo Frugifero...(to) The fruitful age.

Saeculum Novum...The new age.

Sal Gen Hum...Salus Generis Humani (Lasting health to all humans).

Salus DD NN Aug et Caes...The health of Augustus and Caesar, our lords.

Salus Reipublicae...The health of the Republic.

Sanct Deo Soli Elagabal...(to) Holy Sun-God Elagabalus.

Sarmatia Devicta...Victory over Sarmatia.

Securit Imperii...Security of the empire.

Securit Perp...Eternal security.

Serapi Comiti Aug...(to) Serapis, Companion and god of the emperor.

Soli Invicto Comiti...(to) The unconquerable Sun-God.

Senatus Populusque Romanus...The senate and the Roman people.

Inscription   **Liberal Meaning**

SPQR Optimo Principi...The senate and the Roman people to the highest prince.
Spes Perpetua...Eternal hope.
Spes Romanorum...Hope of the Romans.
Summus Sacerdos Aug...Highest prince (or priest) Augustus.
Tempor Felix...The happy times.
Tiberis...The Tiber (A personification).
Ubertas...Fertility.
Undique Victores...Victory everywhere.
Urbs Roma Felix...The happy city, Rome.
Veneri Victrici...(to) Venus the Victress.
Venus Coelestis...Heavenly Venus.
Venus Felix...Happy Venus.
Victoria Aeterna Aug N...Eternal Victory for our emperor.
Victoriae DD Augg NN...(to) Victory of our emperors.
Virtus Exerciti...Referring to the courage of the army.
Virtus Militum...Victory (Virtue) of the army.
Virtus Romanorum...Virtue of the Romans.
Vot Susc or Vota Suscepta...Sacrifice vows.
Votis Decennalibus...Vows of the ten years, or the tenth year.
Vota Publica...Public vows.

Mint Marks

Roman coins began to carry mint marks around the middle of the third century A.D. With the use of these mint marks the emperor had reasonably strict control over the actions of the mint officials. Coins of inadequate weight (perhaps indicating that a mint official was filling his personal purse) were then easily traced to the guilty person or persons.

The mint mark is found in the exergue (bottom) of the reverse. Generally, it consists of three parts: a letter indicating pecunia (p), money, or SM (Sacred money), or M (Moneta). The next letter or letters would indicate the place where the coin was struck. (ROM, Rome; SIR, Sirmium; etc.). Last, the symbol, either in Greek or Latin, indicating the workshop in that particular place. As an example, if the Greek system was used, the first letters of the Greek alphabet (Alpha, Beta, Gamma, etc.) would be found upon the coin, indicating the particular workshop. Workshop number 1 would be Alpha; workshop number 2, Beta; and so on. The Latin system would be used in exactly the same manner and so Prima would be workshop number 1; secunda, workshop number 2; tertia, workshop number 3. The symbols, in this instance, would be "P" for prima, "S" for secunda, and "T" for tertia.

The following list includes some of the more common mints. The names of modern towns appear in parentheses.

Alexandria (*Egypt*)...Al, Ale, Alex.
Ambianum (*Amiens, France*)...Amb, Ambi.
Antioch (*Antikiya, Syria*)...An, Ant.
Aquileia (*Aquileja, Italy*)...Aq, Aqvi.
Arelatum (*Arles, France*)...Ar, Arl.
Camulodunum (*Colchester, Eng.*)...C.
Carthage (*Ruins near Tunis, North Africa*)...K, Kar, Kart.

Constantinople (*Istanbul, Turkey*)...C, Con, Cons, Kon, Kons, Konst.
Cyzicus (*Kapu Dagh, Turkey*)...Cuz, Cuzic, Cyz, Cyzic, K, Kv, Kvz, Ky.
Heraclea (*Eregli, Turkey*)...H, Her, Heracl, Ht, Htr.
Londinium (*London*)...L, Ll, Ln, Lon.
Lugdunum (*Lyons, France*)...Ld, Lg, Lug, Lugd.
Mediolanum (*Milan, Italy*)...Md, Med.
Nicomedia (*Izmit, Turkey*)...N, Nic, Mico, Nik.
Narbo (*Narbonne, France*)...Nar.
Ostia (*The port of Rome*)...Ost.
Ravenna (*Ravenna, Italy*)...Rav.
Rome...R, Rm, Rom, Roma, Urb Rom.
Serdica (*Sophia, Bulgaria*)...Sd, Ser, Serd.
Sirmium (*Ruins near Mitrovica, Yugoslavia*)...Sir, Sirm.
Siscia (*Sisak, Yugoslavia*)...S, Sis, Sisc, Sm.
Thessalonica (*Greece*)...TE, Tes, Th, Ts, Oes.
Ticinum (*Pavia, Italy*)...T.
Treveri (*Trier, France*)...Tr, Tre.

*Antoninianus
struck in
Constantinople*

Note CONS in exergue (bottom) of coin illustrated.

Chronological Sketches
of the Emperors,
Their Contemporaries and Families

Any attempt to tell the story of Rome's Emperors in as brief a manner as is here presented is obviously quite inadequate. However, these little sketches should be of benefit for a hurried background to the collector who is not familiar with the history of Rome. The coins themselves, after all, are but little metal manifestations of the greater story ... the story of Rome itself.

It is impossible to escape the joy, the tragedy, the violence, and the monumental egoism of the people whose hands guided the destinies of millions of Romans.

We read of the tragedy of the emperor-father who committed suicide upon learning of the death of his son in battle. (Gordianus Africanus.) The moral concept of our time forces us to cringe at the alleged sins of Tiberius or the insane depravity of Caligula, who thought to make his horse consul. The great promise which Domitian showed in his early years turned into a disappointing performance of excessive corruption. How did the pupil of the philosopher Seneca (Nero) learn his lessons to become so imbued with evil that he destroyed almost everyone who surrounded him including the mother whose wiles had elevated him to his high position (Agrippina), and a wife (Poppaea)? Even his teacher suffered a similar fate. Assassination, here, reached a high artistic standard.

Do we understand this woman who was mother of an emperor, wife of an emperor, and sister of an emperor? Her ambition brought her the ultimate in every material phase but her actions disgusted even her dissolute son whom she had made emperor. He ordered her to be poisoned. (Agrippina, mother of Nero, wife of the emperor Claudius, sister of the emperor Caligula.)

How low the tides of government had sunk when that very government had to be auctioned to the person who was the highest bidder. Didius Julianus achieved this dubious distinction only to meet a violent death shortly thereafter. And the emperor Marius; little is known of him because he ruled for about two or three days. There was a child-emperor, too. Valentinianus II was proclaimed emperor at the age of 3, not an age to be able to decide whether such a title was to his advantage. He was murdered in his twentieth year.

We read about the boy-ruler. Emperor at the age of 14 and 4 years later dragged, dead, through the streets of Rome to be thrown into the Tiber. Despite his extreme youth he rapidly matured in the fine art of vicious cruelty. (Elagabalus.)

We wonder about the man who thought enough of the throne to wage battle for it but who, upon achieving his ambition, concerned himself more with the luxuries of his table. His fate was to be seized in his palace and to be dragged ignominiously through the streets of Rome to be killed by the mob. (Vitellius.)

What do we say of Commodus? Commodus, the son of the noble and good Marcus Aurelius; Commodus, in whom the sons of Rome had implacable faith that the excellent government of his father would be continued. He answered this faith placed in him by a rule of terror, evil, and corruption. Fate kept an accurate record, however, and his last moments were ruthlessly pressed out of him as he died by strangulation at the hands of an underling.

Fratricide was the peculiar talent possessed by Caracalla. It did not please him to have to share the empire with his brother Geta although it was his father's expressed wish that he do so. And so he had his brother murdered. As if this were not enough he ordered, in addition, that all effigies of his brother . . . on monuments and coins be destroyed. That this was not carried out is indicated by the existence of an abundance of coins of Geta. Caracalla was, himself, murdered.

Yet, there are softer pages as well.

There was a time, a pitifully short time, indeed, when the fortunes of men were guided by the excellent and wise hands of a Nerva, Trajan, Hadrian, Antoninus Pius, and Marcus Aurelius. These few 80 some-odd years saw peace predominate and Sagacity upon the throne.

Your coins will have a greater meaning if you pursue this magnificent story of a people, without whom there would have been no coins . . . and not much of anything.

Chronological Sketches of the Most Prominent Emperors, Their Families and Contemporaries

Augustus

AUGUSTUS—Gaius (or Caius) Julius Caesar Octavianus. First Roman emperor. Great nephew of Julius Caesar who adopted him as heir to the throne. Joined Mark Anthony and Lepidus in forming the Second Triumvirate. Received the title of Augustus from the senate. Ruler of the Roman world in 29 BC. Died in 14 AD at the age of 77.

Livia

LIVIA—Wife of Tiberius Claudius Nero by whom she had two children: Tiberius, later emperor, and Nero Claudius Drusus. Was forced by Augustus to divorce her husband and marry him. Died in 29 AD at the probable age of 85.

Agrippa

AGRIPPA—Marcus Vipsanius Agrippa. Roman general. A close friend of Augustus and his heir. Predeceased the emperor, however, in 12 BC at the age of 51.

Julia

JULIA—Daughter of Augustus. Born 39 BC. Her profligacies forced her father to banish her. She was the wife of the following: Marcellus, Agrippa, and the emperor Tiberius. Died in 14 AD at the age of 53.

CAIUS AND LUCIUS CAESARS—Sons of Agrippa and Julia. Caius died 4 AD, Lucius, 2 AD.

Caius and Lucius Caesars

TIBERIUS—Tiberius Claudius Nero. The 2nd Roman emperor. Reigned during the time of Christ. Was a just and kind ruler at first, (he became emperor at the death of Augustus who adopted him after the death of Agrippa) but allegedly became base and cruel. Much of this due to the evil influence of Sejanus, Prefect of the Praetorian Guard. He was born in 42 BC, became emperor in 14 AD and died at Capri, where he spent the last 10 years of his life, in the year of 37 AD.

Tiberius

DRUSUS, JR.—Born 14 or 15 BC, died 23 AD. Son of emperor Tiberius and Vipsania. His wife Livilla was seduced by Sejanus and these two successfully plotted the death, by poisoning, of Drusus.

Drusus, Jr.

NERO CLAUDIUS DRUSUS—Brother of Tiberius and father of emperor Claudius. Died in 9 BC, reputedly as a result of being thrown by his horse.

Nero Claudius Drusus

ANTONIA—Daughter of Marc Anthony and Octavia. Grandmother of the emperor Nero. She was about 77 years of age at her death.

Antonia

[63

Germanicus

GERMANICUS—Son of Nero Claudius Drusus. Nephew of the emperor Tiberius. A great popular favorite. Died near Antioch in 19 AD possibly by poisoning under orders from Tiberius.

Agrippina the Elder

AGRIPPINA THE ELDER—Daughter of Agrippa and Julia (daughter of Augustus), wife of Germanicus and mother of the emperor Caligula. After the death of her husband she was banished to the island of Pandataria where she died in 33 AD at the probable age of 46.

Nero and Drusus Caesars

NERO AND DRUSUS CAESARS—Sons of Germanicus and Agrippina. Nero died in 31 AD, Drusus in 33 AD.

Caligula

CALIGULA—Caius Caesar. Roman emperor, 37-41 AD. Youngest son of Germanicus and Agrippina. From his association with the soldiers in his youth when he wore the Roman boots called caligae, he was named Caligula (little boot). As heir to Tiberius, he ruled with reasonableness at first, but soon became excessively depraved and cruel. He was undoubtedly insane and even thought to name his horse Consul. He was assassinated by the Praetorian guard in 41 AD, at the age of 29.

CAESONIA—Fourth wife of Caligula. Murdered with her husband.

DRUSILLA—Sister of Caligula. Daughter of Germanicus and Agrippina.

CLAUDIUS—Tiberius Claudius Drusus. Roman emperor 41-54 AD. Son of Nero Claudius Drusus and Antonia. Became emperor by acclamation of the legions upon the death of Caligula. Married four times, his most prominent wives being Messalina, and his niece, the younger Agrippina, who was the mother of the future emperor Nero. She had Claudius adopt her son Nero to the disadvantage of his own son, Brittanicus. Her cruelty reached the highest extreme when she had Claudius poisoned in the year 54 AD. He was 64 years of age.

AGRIPPINA THE YOUNGER—She was the mother of an emperor (Nero), the sister of an emperor (Caligula), daughter of Germanicus and Agrippina. Noted for her excessive cruelties, she was the vicious daughter of a noble and fine mother. After poisoning her husband, the emperor Claudius, she, in turn, was assassinated by agents of her son Nero in 59 AD. She was 44.

BRITTANICUS—Tiberius Claudius Brittanicus. Son of Claudius and Messalina. Having been set aside as the logical heir to the throne due to the intercession of Agrippina Junior on behalf of her own son Nero, he was subsequently poisoned by Nero in 55 AD at the age of 13 or 14.

Caesonia

Drusilla

Claudius

Agrippina the Younger

Brittanicus

Nero

Poppaea

Clodius Macer

Galba

NERO—Nero Claudius Caesar Drusus Germanicus. Roman emperor 54-68 AD. The first part of Nero's reign was uneventful. What happened thereafter is history which seems to be known by most schoolboys. He became a terror to the noble families of Rome; poisoned Brittanicus, his predecessor's son, poisoned his own mother and even his famous tutor, the philosopher Seneca. He was accused of setting the great fire at Rome and persecuted the Christians because he needed scapegoats for this act. He was finally forced to commit suicide in 68 AD at the age of 31.

POPPAEA—Poppaea Sabina. She was the wife of Crispinus and the mistress of Otho. She subsequently divorced Crispinus to marry Otho. Upon this auspicious occasion she became the mistress of the emperor Nero, so she divorced Otho and married Nero. Her ultimate reward was a violent kick by Nero which resulted in her death, probably in 65 AD.

CLODIUS MACER—Lucius Clodius Macer. He was propraetor in Africa during the reign of Nero. Refused to recognize Galba as the new emperor after Nero's death and, as a result, was captured by Galba's troops and killed.

GALBA—Roman emperor for 7 months 68-69 AD. Proclaimed emperor by the praetorian guard after Nero's suicide. His harsh discipline was resented by his soldiers and he was killed by them. He was 63 years of age.

OTHO—Marcus Salvius Otho. Emperor for three months in the year 69 AD. Envious because he was not named Galba's heir, he led an insurrection and after the death of Galba was proclaimed emperor. He was defeated in battle by Vitellius and committed suicide at the age of 37.

Otho

VITELLIUS—Aulus Vitellius. Emperor, Jan. to Dec., 69 AD. His legions proclaimed for him after the death of Galba at the same time Otho's legions declared for Otho. Defeated Otho in battle and was sole emperor for the brief time stated above. The Illyrian legions, meanwhile, declared for Vespasian. Vespasian's forces defeated Vitellius who suffered an ignominious death, afterwards being dragged through the streets by the mob. His banquets, at which he gorged himself, were known far and wide and it was said that if he had paid more attention to affairs of state than to his exploits in eating, he might have survived. He was 54 at his death.

Vitellius

VESPASIAN—Titus Flavius Sabinus Vespasianus. The first of the Flavian emperors. Ruled 69-79 AD. Held various offices and became proconsul in Africa under Nero. His legions declared for him while other legions declared for Otho or Vitellius. After Otho's death Vitellius was disposed of and Vespasian assumed the complete power. He was a competent emperor. He died in 79 AD at the age of 70.

Vespasian

DOMITILLA—First wife of Vespasian. Died before he became emperor. She was the mother of the future emperors Titus and Domitian.

Domitilla

[67

Titus

TITUS—Emperor, 79-81 AD. Son of Vespasian and Domitilla. Known for his subjection of Judaea in the year 70. He led a rather profligate life before becoming emperor, but upon ascending the throne became an efficient emperor. He died in 81 AD at the age of 41.

Julia Titi

JULIA TITI—Daughter of Titus.

Domitian

DOMITIAN—Titus Flavius Domitianus. Second son of Vespasian. Emperor 81-96 AD. The early part of his reign was uneventful, the latter part found him to be insatiably cruel and tyrannical. He was finally murdered, to the obvious relief of all concerned. His wife Domitia was one of the conspirators. He was 45 at his death.

Nerva

NERVA—Marcus Cocceius Nerva. Emperor 96-98 AD. Held responsible offices under Vespasian, Titus, and Domitian. Was consul with Domitian in the year 90 AD. He was the first of the excellent emperors who were to rule for the next eighty some odd years. He died in 98 AD at the age of 66.

TRAJAN—Marcus Ulpius Trajanus. Emperor 98-117. Adopted as Nerva's heir in 97. Under him the Roman Empire reached its greatest geographical extent. He was an excellent emperor. He was 65 at his death in 117.

Trajan

PLOTINA—Wife of Trajan.

Plotina

MARCIANA—Sister of Trajan.

Marciana

MATIDIA—Daughter of Marciana.

Matidia

HADRIAN—Publius Aelius Hadrianus. Emperor 117-138. Nephew of Trajan and his heir. Erected many fine buildings in Rome and elsewhere. He continued the fine government of his two predecessors. Died in 138 at the age of 62.

Hadrian

Sabina

SABINA—Wife of Hadrian. Predeceased him in 137.

Aelius

AELIUS—Lucius Aelius Verus Caesar. Adopted by Hadrian as his heir, but he died in 138.

Antoninus Pius

ANTONINUS PIUS—Titus Aelius Hadrianus Antoninus. (Originally, before his adoption by Hadrian after the death of Aelius his name was Titus Aurelius Fulvus Boionius Arrius.) Emperor 138-161. Enjoyed a peaceful and prosperous reign. Because of this, history has little to record of his rule. He adopted his nephew Marcus Aurelius whom his daughter Faustina had married. 75 years of age at death.

Faustina the Elder

FAUSTINA THE ELDER—Wife of Antoninus Pius. Her full name was Annia Galeria Faustina. Some writers have said that she was noted for her lack of morals. She died in 141 at the age of 37.

MARCUS AURELIUS—Marcus Aelius Aurelius Verus. Emperor, 161-180. Had been adopted by Antoninus Pius as his heir, along with Lucius Verus. Verus was his colleague in government. He was a philosopher and was a step towards the Platonic concept of the philosopher king. His "Meditations" are still extant. He was 69 at his death in 180.

Marcus Aurelius

ANNIUS VERUS—Son of Marcus Aurelius.

Annius Verus

FAUSTINA THE YOUNGER—Wife of Marcus Aurelius, allegedly noted for her lack of morals, although some scholars question this. She died in 175 at the probable age of 50.

Faustina the Younger

LUCIUS VERUS—Lucius Aurelius Verus. Originally Lucius Ceionius Commodus. Colleague of Marcus Aurelius. Had been adopted by Antoninus Pius as had been Marcus Aurelius. Died in 169 at the age of 39.

Lucius Verus

LUCILLA—Wife of Lucius Verus and sister of Commodus who, when he became emperor, had her murdered in 183.

Lucilla

Commodus

COMMODUS — Lucius Aelius Aurelius Commodus. The abrupt halt to a happy era. The dissolute son of a noble father, he was emperor from 180-192. His reign was a retrogression to all of the evil which existed before Nerva. Cruel, intemperate, and prodigal, he was finally strangled to death while in a drunken stupor. He was 31 years of age at his death.

Crispina

CRISPINA—Wife of Commodus. He had her killed.

Pertinax

PERTINAX—Publius Helvius Pertinax. Emperor in year 193. He was chosen emperor against his will after the death of Commodus. Certain reforms instituted by him met with disfavor and the reactionary element of the praetorian guard murdered him in 193. He was 67 at his death.

Didius Julianus

DIDIUS JULIANUS—Marcus Didius Salvius Julianus (or Severus Julianus). Ruled about three months in the year 193. The most notable thing about this emperor was the fact that he purchased the throne at auction, an indication of how low the tides of empire had fallen. He was almost immediately unpopular and was slain. He was 60 years of age at his death.

Manlia Scantilla

MANLIA SCANTILLA—Wife of Didius Julianus.

DIDIA CLARA — Daughter of Didius Julianus.

Didia Clara

PESCENNIUS NIGER—Caius Pescennius Niger. Proclaimed emperor by the Syrian legions. The armies of Severus defeated him and he fled only to be subsequently captured and put to death along with all the members of his family, in 194.

Pescennius Niger

CLODIUS ALBINUS—Decimus Clodius Ceionius Septimius Albinus. Elevated to Caesar under Severus, but after Severus defeated Niger he had the senate declare Albinus a public enemy. After a battle near Lyons, Albinus was defeated and slain in 197.

Clodius Albinus

SEPTIMIUS SEVERUS—Lucius Septimius Severus. Emperor, 193-211. Held important posts under Marcus Aurelius. Declared against Julianus and Niger, as well as Albinus and assumed the supreme control. He was 65 at his death in 211.

Septimius Severus

JULIA DOMNA—Wife of the emperor Severus, mother of the emperors Caracalla and Geta. Was a person of considerable intellect. She committed suicide after the death of Caracalla, in 217. She was about 50 at her death.

Julia Domna

Caracalla

CARACALLA—Marcus Aurelius Antoninus. Original name, Bassianus. Emperor 211-217. Son of the emperor Severus. Caracalla was a nickname given to him because of the long coat known by that name which he introduced to Rome from Gaul. He was, at first, joint emperor with his brother Geta, but he convinced the praetorian guard to name him sole emperor. He had his brother murdered and, according to some sources, some twenty thousand others as well. He was a treacherous, worthless profligate who was finally murdered by Macrinus. He was 29 years of age at his death in 217.

Plautilla

PLAUTILLA—Wife of Caracalla.

Geta

GETA—Lucius Septimius Geta. Younger son of Severus. Joint ruler with his brother Caracalla (209-212). However, the desire on the part of Caracalla for supreme and sole power caused him to have Geta murdered, and all effigies, coins, and other permanent works with the image of Geta destroyed. Geta was 23 years of age when he was murdered.

Macrinus

MACRINUS—Marcus Opelius Severus Macrinus. Emperor 217-218. Instrumental in the death of Caracalla. The Parthians, in revolt, defeated him. He became unpopular with the army and was subsequently slain in 218 at the age of 54.

DIADUMENIAN—Marcus Opelius Antoninus Diadumenianus. Son of Macrinus. Killed in the revolt which resulted in his father's death.

Diadumenian

ELAGABALUS or HELIOGABALUS—Marcus Aurelius Antoninus. Originally, Varius Avitus Bassianus. Emperor 218-222. He was a priest in the temple of the sun-god (thus his name, Helio-Sun) at Emesa. Defeated Macrinus in battle and then went on to practice extreme debaucheries and cruelties. He was slain by the praetorian guard at the age of 18, dragged along the streets with his mother who also had been slain, and thrown unceremoniously into the Tiber.

Elagabalus or Heliogabalus

JULIA PAULA—First wife of Elagabalus. He divorced her after a year of marriage.

Julia Paula

AQUILIA SEVERA—Second wife of Elagabalus. He divorced her, but returned to her after divorcing his third wife, Annia Faustina.

Aquilia Severa

ANNIA FAUSTINA—Third wife of Elagabalus. Divorced her and returned to his second wife, Aquilia Severa.

Annia Faustina

Julia Soaemias

JULIA SOAEMIAS—Mother of Elagabalus. Murdered with him.

Julia Maesa

JULIA MAESA—Grandmother of Elagabalus.

Severus Alexander

SEVERUS ALEXANDER—Marcus Aurelius Severus Alexander. Adopted by his cousin Elagabalus as his heir. Ruled from 222-235. He was a just and wise ruler, but was slain by some mutinous soldiers on his way to Germany to subdue a revolt. His mother was slain with him. He was probably 27 years of age at his death.

Orbiana

ORBIANA—Third wife of Severus Alexander.

JULIA MAMAEA—Mother of Severus Alexander. Murdered by mutinous soldiers along with her son in 235.

Julia Mamaea

URANIUS ANTONINUS — Lucius Julius Aurelius Sulpicius Uranius Antoninus. A usurper (235).

MAXIMINUS I—Caius Julius Verus Maximinus. Had the surname, The Thracian. Emperor 235-238. Was supposed to have been of great size and strength. Was declared emperor by the legions of the Rhine after the death of Severus Alexander. He was cruel and tyrannical and was slain by his own soldiers.

Maximinus I

MAXIMUS—Son of Maximinus I. Murdered with his father.

PAULINA—Wife of Maximinus I.

Paulina

GORDIANUS AFRICANUS I—Marcus Antonius Gordianus I. Ruled 36 days in the year 238. Was proconsul in Africa under Severus Alexander. Was proclaimed emperor by his followers in Africa and was confirmed by the senate when Maximinus was declared to be a public enemy by that same body. He committed suicide when he learned of the death of his son in battle with one of the supporters of Maximinus. He was 80 years of age at his death.

Gordianus Africanus I

Gordianus Africanus II

GORDIANUS AFRICANUS II—Marcus Antonianus Gordianus II. Son of Gordianus I. Associated with his father as co-emperor. Killed in battle at Carthage by Capellianus, the governor of Numidia.

Balbinus

BALBINUS—Decimus Caelius Balbinus. Emperor for about two months in the year 238. He was proclaimed joint emperor by the senate along with Pupienus Maximus, essentially to oppose Maximinus who was threatening Rome. Maximinus was slain, however, and Balbinus was murdered by the Praetorian guard.

Pupienus

PUPIENUS—Marcus Clodius Pupienus Maximus. Appointed joint emperor with Balbinus to oppose Maximinus who threatened Rome. Pupienus was slain by the Praetorian guard, along with Balbinus, after a reign of about two months.

Gordianus III (Pius)

GORDIANUS III (PIUS)—Marcus Antonius Gordianus. He was the grandson of Gordianus I. Proclaimed Caesar during the reign of Balbinus and Pupienus. At their deaths proclaimed emperor by the Praetorian guard at the age of 14 or 15. He ruled for six years (238-244) and through the manipulations of Philippus, an officer of the guard, he was murdered at the age of 21. Philippus succeeded him to the throne.

TRANQUILLINA — Wife of Gordianus III.

Tranquillina

PHILIP I — Marcus Julius Philippus. An officer of the Praetorian guard during the reign of Gordianus Pius. As a result of his machinations, Gordianus was slain. Philip was himself killed battling the legions of Trajan Decius. He was emperor from 244-249.

Philip I

OTACILIA SEVERA — Marcia Otacilia Severa. Wife of Philip I.

Otacilia Severa

PHILIP II—Marcus Julius Severus Philippus. Son of Philip I. Was murdered soon after his father.

PACATIAN—A usurper about whom very little is known (249).

Philip II

JOTAPIAN — A Syrian usurper about whom little is known (249?).

Jotapian

[79

Trajan Decius

TRAJAN DECIUS—Caius Messius Quintus Traianus Decius. Emperor 249-251. Was commander of the troops of Danube during the reign of Philip I. His soldiers revolted against Philip and he was forced to become emperor by them against his will. He defeated Philip in battle and Philip was killed. Decius was slain in Thrace battling the Goths. He was 53 years of age at his death.

Etruscilla

ETRUSCILLA—Wife of Trajan Decius.

Herennius Etruscus

HERENNIUS ETRUSCUS—Quintus Herennius Etruscus Messius Decius. Son of Trajan Decius and killed at the same time as his father.

Hostilian

HOSTILIAN—Caius Valens Hostilianus Messius Quintus. A younger son of Trajan Decius about whom little is known.

Trebonianus Gallus

TREBONIANUS GALLUS—Caius Vibius Trebonianus Gallus. Emperor 251-254. Appointed to serve as Hostilian's associate. He effected a peace with the Goths which was felt to be degrading by the Romans. He was subsequently murdered by his own soldiers.

VOLUSIAN—Caius Vibius Volusianus Trebonianus Asinius. Son of Trebonianus Gallus. Killed at the same time as his father.

Volusian

AEMILIAN — Marcus Aemilius Aemilianus. (253-254.) A governor of Pannonia and Moesia during the reign of Gallus. He was hailed as emperor by his troops and defeated the forces of Gallus in battle. He was murdered by his own soldiers.

Aemilian

CORNELIA SUPERA—Wife of Aemilian.

Cornelia Supera

VALERIAN—Publius Licinius Valerianus. Emperor 253-260. Of noble birth, he was loyal to Gallus but could give him no help in his battle with Aemilian, arriving too late. At the death of Gallus was proclaimed emperor and associated his son Gallienus with him. Troubles on the borders forced him into many battles. Was defeated by the Persian, Shapuri, and held captive until his death.

Valerian

Mariniana

MARINIANA—Wife of Valerian.

Gallienus

GALLIENUS—Publius Licinius Valerianus Egnatius Gallienus. Son of Valerian. Emperor 253-268. Became sole emperor after the capture of his father by the Persians. He was obliged to deal with disintegration from within the empire and from without. It proved to be too great a task. He was killed by his own soldiers at the age of 50.

Saloninus

SALONINUS—Son of Gallienus. Killed by Postumus in 259 AD.

Salonina

SALONINA—Wife of Gallienus.

Valerian II

VALERIAN II—Son of Gallienus. Died about 255.

MACRIANUS I — Marcus Fulvius Macrianus. (260-261.) It was due to his incompetence that the Roman army of Valerian was defeated, resulting in the capture of the emperor. Nevertheless, Macrianus was declared emperor by his troops. On his way back to Italy he was met in battle by one of Valerian's generals and was defeated and slain.

Macrianus I

MACRIANUS II—Titus Fulvius Julius Macrianus. (260-261.) Son of Macrianus. Slain at the same time as his father.

Macrianus II

QUIETUS—Fulvius Julius Quietus. (260-261.) Youngest son of Macrianus I. When his father left for Rome after the Eastern campaign, he was left to administer affairs. He was attacked by the king of the Palmyrans, defeated, captured, and killed.

Quietus

REGALIANUS—Publius Caius Regalianus. (260-261.) A general under Valerian. At Valerian's death, he seized the power in Pannonia but was killed shortly thereafter.

DRYANTILLA—Wife of Regalianus.

Regalianus

POSTUMUS—Marcus Cassianus Latinus Postumus. Emperor 259-267. Governor of Gaul under Valerian. After declaring himself emperor during the reign of Valerian, he ruled in Britain and in Gaul. He was a wise ruler but was killed in battle as a result of his usurpations.

Postumus

[83

Laelianus

LAELIANUS—Ulpius Cornelius Laelianus (267). Led a revolt against Postumus and was killed.

Victorinus

VICTORINUS—Marcus Piavvonius Victorinus. (265-270?) Sole ruler of Gaul after having been co-emperor with Postumus. Assassinated by his own soldiers.

Marius

MARIUS—Caius Marcus Aurelius Marius (268). Proclaimed himself emperor at the death of Postumus, but was killed almost immediately, probably within a few days.

Tetricus I

TETRICUS I—C Pius Esuvius Tetricus. (267-276.) Declared himself emperor and associated his son with him. He finally abdicated and, strange as it seems, was allowed to live out his days in Rome.

Tetricus II

TETRICUS II—Caius Pius Esuvius Tetricus. (272-276.) Son of Tetricus the Elder and associated with his father in his father's rule. He was spared death upon the abdication of his father and himself after being defeated by Aurelian at Chalons.

Claudius II Gothicus

CLAUDIUS II GOTHICUS—Marcus Aurelius Claudius. Emperor 268-270. Possessed an excellent military record under Decius, Valerian and Gallienus. Fought two great battles; against the Alamanni in northern Italy and the Goths in Moesia from which he obtained the title "Gothicus." He died during a plague in the year 270 at the age of 56.

QUINTILLUS—Caius Marcus Aurelius Claudius Quintillus. Emperor 270. Supported as emperor at the death of Claudius, but the legions of Sirmium declared for Aurelian. He ultimately committed suicide.

Quintillus

AURELIAN—Lucius Domitius Aurelianus. Emperor 270-275. Known as Restitutor Orbis (Restorer of the Empire). Occupied high military positions under Valerian and Claudius II. Pushed Goths across the Danube; defeated Palmyra and brought the queen, Zenobia, back to Rome; reconquered Egypt; fortified Rome. He was murdered as a result of a conspiracy at the age of 63.

Aurelian

SEVERINA—Wife of Aurelian.

Severina

VABALATHUS—Son of Zenobia, queen of Palmyra. Ruler of that state under his mother's tutelage.

Vabalathus

ZENOBIA—Queen of Palmyra. Captured by Aurelian and brought to Rome. She was eventually pardoned and allowed to live in Italy.

Zenobia

Tacitus

TACITUS—Marcus Claudius Tacitus. Emperor 275-276. Elected by the senate after the death of Aurelian. Claimed descent from the famous historian. Ruled for about six months. Was killed by his soldiers at the age of 76.

Florianus

FLORIANUS—Marcus Annius Florianus. Emperor for a few weeks in 276. Seized power at the death of his half brother Tacitus. Opposed by Probus and killed in battle.

Probus

PROBUS—Marcus Aurelius Probus. Emperor 276-282. Was governor of the east under Tacitus after serving in a distinguished manner in the armies of Valerian, Claudius and Aurelian. Initiated many beneficial improvements in government, but he was killed by mutinous soldiers.

Carus

CARUS—Marcus Aurelius Carus. Emperor 282-283. Prefect of the praetorian guard under Probus. At the death of Probus chosen emperor by the soldiers. Appointed his sons, Carinus and Numerian, as Caesars. While fighting the Persians he was killed, either in battle, or, according to some versions, struck by lightning.

CARINUS—Marcus Aurelius Carinus. Emperor 283-285. Eldest son of Carus. Appointed governor of the western provinces while his father and brother Numerian proceeded against the Persians. Defeated Diocletian in battle, but was murdered by one of his own officers.

Carinus

MAGNIA URBICA—Wife of Carinus.

Magnia Urbica

NIGRINIAN—Possibly a son of Carinus.

Nigrinian

NUMERIAN—Marcus Aurelius Numerianus. Emperor 283-284, jointly with his brother Carinus. He died shortly after his father, Carus.

Numerian

JULIAN—Marcus Aurelius Julianus. A rebellious general who served under the emperor Carinus. He was slain in 285.

Julian

Diocletian

DIOCLETIAN—Caius Aurelius Valerius Diocletianus. Emperor 284-305. Born at Dioclea in Dalmatia from whence his name was derived. Held commands under Probus, Aurelian, and Carus. Was proclaimed emperor at the death of Numerian. Was associated with Maximianus I, and later with Galerius and Constantius Chlorus. Viciously persecuted the Christians, but on the other hand, he did much to reform the internal affairs of the empire. He abdicated in 305 and lived out his life in retirement. He was 68 at his death.

Maximianus I (Herculius)

MAXIMIANUS I (HERCULIUS)—Marcus Aurelius Valerius Maximianus. Emperor 286-305. Born in Pannonia of humble origin. Was associated with the emperor Diocletian. He abdicated with Diocletian (305) but returned to champion the cause of his son, Maxentius, who had claimed the throne in opposition to Galerius and Constantius. Because of complicity in a plot against Constantine, he was ordered to end his own life.

Carausius

CARAUSIUS—Marcus Aurelius Mausaeus Carausius. Usurper in Britain (287-293). Was in command of the fleet in northern Gaul, but taking advantage of his position, he turned to indiscriminate plunder and fell into disfavor. Fled to Britain and proclaimed himself emperor. He was defeated by the fleet of Maximian and was slain by his chief minister Allectus. He was probably 48 years old at his death.

Allectus

ALLECTUS—Caius Allectus. The chief minister of Carausius, he was the cause of the latter's death. Declared himself emperor and ruled cruelly (293-296). The legions of Constantius killed him in a battle in Britain.

CONSTANTIUS I (CHLORUS)—Flavius Valerius Constantius. Caesar 295-305; Augustus 305-306. Son-in-law of Maximian, father of Constantine the Great. Adopted as Caesar by Maximian. Upon abdication of Diocletian and Maximian assumed full power. He died in 306, at the age of 56.

Constantius I (Chlorus)

HELENA—Wife of Constantius I. Mother of Constantine the Great.

Helena

GALERIUS—Caius Galerius Valerius Maximianus. Caesar, 293-305; Augustus, 305-311. Created Caesar by Diocletian. Was beaten by the Persians, but subsequently inflicted a great defeat upon them. Extremely inimical to the Christians and probably had much to do with persuading Diocletian to persecute them. As emperor he elevated Licinius to the rank of Caesar. He died in 311.

Galerius

GALERIA VALERIA—Daughter of Diocletian; second wife of Galerius.

Galeria Valeria

SEVERUS II—Flavius Valerius Severus. Caesar, 305-306; Augustus, 306-307. Created Caesar by Galerius who also named him Augustus. He was unsuccessful in battle with Maxentius and was forced to commit suicide.

Severus II

Maxentius

MAXENTIUS—Marcus Aurelius Valerius Maxentius. Son of Maximian. Emperor 306-312. Not being a particularly admirable person he was passed over when his father and Diocletian appointed the new Caesars. Led an uprising and was proclaimed Caesar by the praetorian guard. He overthrew Severus and drove Galerius from Italy. Attacked Constantine and suffered a complete defeat. He drowned while fleeing across the Tiber.

ROMULUS—Son of Maxentius.

Romulus

ALEXANDER—A usurper in Africa. Governor of that province under Maxentius. Proclaimed himself emperor, but was crushed almost immediately.

Alexander

MAXIMINUS II (DAZA)—Galerius Valerius Maximinus. Maximinus was a nephew of the emperor Galerius and was made Caesar in 305 at which time he governed Egypt and Syria. Became emperor in 308 and was defeated by Licinius. He died in 314.

Maximinus II (Daza)

Licinius I

LICINIUS I—Publius Flavius Galerius Valerius Licianus Licinius. Emperor 307-324. Given the rank of Augustus by Galerius. He married a half-sister of Constantine the Great and with him issued the edict of Milan recognizing Christianity. He and Maximinus Daza agreed to rule jointly. Maximinus, however, attacked him and was defeated. There was not lasting amity between Licinius and Constantine and in making war upon Constantine, Licinius was seized and slain. He was probably 55 years of age at his death.

LICINIUS II—Flavius Valerius Licinius Licinius. Son of Licinius I. He was put to death, shortly after his father, at the age of 9.

Licinius II

VALENS—Aurelius Valerius Valens. Created Augustus (314) by Licinius but murdered shortly thereafter.

MARTINIAN—Marcus Martinianus. Created Augustus by Licinius (323). Seized and put to death with the latter.

Valens

CONSTANTINE I (THE GREAT)—Flavius Valerius Aurelius Constantinus. Caesar, 306-308; Augustus, 308-337. Son of Constantius Chlorus. At the time he was proclaimed Caesar by his father there were five claimants to the throne. Defeated Maxentius and then Licinius to secure authority. Devoted much time to internal administration, strengthening of the borders, elimination of abuses. By the Edict of Milan he recognized Christianity. Called the Council of Nicaea (325) where the Nicene Creed was adopted. Chose Byzantium as the new capital of the empire and renamed it Constantinople. He was probably 57 years of age at his death.

Martinian

Constantine I (The Great)

THEODORA—Flavia Maxima Theodora. Second wife of Constantius Chlorus.

Fausta

FAUSTA—Flavia Maxima Fausta. Wife of Constantine the Great and daughter of Maximianus Herculius.

Crispus

CRISPUS—Flavius Julius Crispus. Son of Constantine the Great. He was a great popular favorite and this possibly was, in part, the cause of his death, by his father's orders. He was Caesar from 317-326.

Delmatius

DELMATIUS—Flavius Julius Delmatius. Nephew of Constantine the Great. Caesar 335-337. Murdered after the death of Constantine.

Hanniballianus

HANNIBALLIANUS—Flavius Claudius Hanniballianus. Caesar, 335-337. Murdered along with his brother Delmatius. They were nephews of Constantine.

Constantine II

CONSTANTINE II—Flavius Claudius Julius Constantinus. Son of Constantine the Great. Emperor 337-340. Joint emperor with his brothers Constantius and Constans at his father's death. In warring with Constans he was killed.

CONSTANS—Flavius Julius Constans. Caesar, 333-337. Augustus, 337-350. His share of the empire at the death of Constantine the Great consisted of Italy, Africa, and Illyricum. In war with his brothers he defeated and killed Constantine II. Later, Magnentius attacked him and Constans was overtaken while fleeing and was killed.

Constans

CONSTANTIUS II—Flavius Julius Constantius. Caesar, 323-337; Augustus, 337-361. Son of Constantine and Fausta. Defeated Magnentius after having become sole ruler at the death of Constans. The empire enjoyed a few years of peace during his reign. However, he learned that his cousin Julian had proclaimed himself emperor and in moving to crush this usurper he died at the age of 44.

Constantius II

CONSTANTIUS GALLUS—Flavius Claudius Constantius. A nephew of Constantine the Great, who usurped the power in the east. His rule of oppression brought him to trial and he was executed (354.)

Constantius Gallus

NEPOTIAN—Flavius Popilius Nepotianus Constantius. Emperor for a brief time in 350. A nephew of Constantine the Great. He seized the throne of Constans, but was killed almost immediately in a battle with Magnentius.

Nepotian

VETRANIO—Proclaimed emperor by his troops at the death of Constans. After a reign of less than a year (350-351) he retired and lived out his years in peace.

Vetranio

Magnentius

MAGNENTIUS—Flavius Popilius Magnentius. Emperor 350-353. Of barbarian birth, he was in command of the troops of the Rhine. Caused the death of Constans and was proclaimed emperor. He was defeated by Constantius II and fled to Gaul where he committed suicide.

Decentius

DECENTIUS—Magnus Decentius. Brother of Magnentius. Upon hearing of the suicide of his brother he, too, committed suicide (353).

Julian II

JULIAN II—Flavius Claudius Julianus. Emperor 361-363. Known as Julian the Apostate because of his paganism and aversion to Christianity. Well educated. He was the brother of Julius Constantius who was a half-brother of Constantine the Great. Proclaimed emperor by his troops in a revolt against the latter. At the death of Constantius he became sole ruler. He was killed during one of his battles with the Persians. He was 32 years of age at his death.

Helena

HELENA—Daughter of Constantine the Great and wife of Julian II.

Jovian

JOVIAN—Flavius Claudius Jovianus. Emperor 363-364. General of army under Julian. Proclaimed emperor by his soldiers after the death of the latter. Made an unhappy peace with the Persians by giving up the provinces beyond the Tigris. Supported the Nicene Creed; restored privileges to the Christians. Died an obscure death in Galatia. He was probably 33 years of age at his death.

VALENTINIAN I—Flavius Valentinianus. Emperor 364-375. Of poor parentage, he entered the army and moved swiftly through the ranks. Held in disfavor by both Constantius and Julian (the latter banished him). At the death of Jovian chosen emperor; appointed Valens, his brother, as associate. His reign knew the encroachments of many barbarian tribes. Died in 375 at the age of 54.

Valentinian I

VALENS—Younger brother of Valentinian I. Made emperor of the east by his brother. Waged war unsuccessfully against the Goths. Made a disgraceful treaty with the Persians. He was subsequently defeated and slain by the Goths. Was emperor from 364-378. He was about 50 years of age at his death.

Valens

PROCOPIUS—A usurper who rebelled against Valens. He was executed (366).

Procopius

GRATIAN—Flavius Gratianus. Emperor 375-383. Son of Valentinian I. He and a brother, Valentinian II, were joint Augusti of the west. At the defeat of Valens also became emperor in the east, with Theodosius as his colleague. Killed in battle with Magnus Maximus at the age of 24.

Gratian

VALENTINIAN II—Son of Valentinian I and younger brother of Gratian. Emperor, jointly with his brother (375-383). Emperor until 392. He was 3 years of age when proclaimed emperor, under the guardianship of the Empress Justina. He was murdered by one of his generals, Arbogast, at the age of 20.

Valentinian II

Theodosius I (The Great)

THEODOSIUS I (THE GREAT)—Flavius Theodosius. Emperor 379-395. Summoned to serve as associate by Gratian at the death of Valens. A cruel ruler, he died at Milan, after having made his sons, Honorius and Arcadius, Caesars. He was about 50 at his death.

Aelia Flaccilla

AELIA FLACCILLA—Wife of Theodosius I.

Magnus Maximus

MAGNUS MAXIMUS—Magnus Clemens Maximus. Emperor 383-388. Declared emperor by his soldiers who did not favor Gratian. He defeated Gratian in battle, but subsequently met with Theodosius who had him executed.

Flavius Victor

FLAVIUS VICTOR (387-388)—Son of Magnus Maximus. He was defeated fighting the Franks in Gaul, taken prisoner and executed.

Eugenius

EUGENIUS—Proclaimed emperor after the murder of Valentinian II. Captured and slain by Theodosius (394).

HONORIUS—Flavius Honorius. Emperor of the west, 395-423. Second son of Theodosius the Great. His reign was one of constant turmoil due to attacks by the Visigoths under Alaric. Roman power suffered a severe decline under this inept rule. He was 39 at his death.

Honorius

ARCADIUS—Emperor (395-408.) Son of Theodosius I. Affairs of state did not interest him and the government was ruled by others. Alaric, the Goth, ruled at this time in what is now the Balkan region. He died in 408 at the age of 31.

Arcadius

CONSTANTIUS III—Emperor 421. Roman general raised to rank of Augustus by Honorius. Reigned only seven months.

Constantius III

GALLA PLACIDA—Daughter of Theodosius the Great.

Galla Placida

CONSTANTINE III—Usurper in Gaul and Britain. (407-411.)

CONSTANS—Son of Constantine III. (408-411).

Constantine III

Maximus

MAXIMUS—Usurper in Spain. Publicly executed by Honorius. (409-411.)

Jovinus

JOVINUS—Usurper in Gaul. Killed by the Goths. (411-413.)

SEBASTIANUS (412-413)—Brother of Jovinus. Killed with him.

Priscus Attalus

PRISCUS ATTALUS—Usurper in Gaul. (409-410.)

Johannes

JOHANNES—Proclaimed himself emperor after the death of Honorius. Defeated by Theodosius. (423-425.)

Valentinian III

VALENTINIAN III—Son of Constantius III. Murdered. (425-455.)

PETRONIUS MAXIMUS—Named emperor after the death of Valentinian III. Murdered within a few months. (455.)

LICINIA EUDOXIA—Daughter of Theodosius II. Wife of Valentinian III.

Petronius Maximus

AVITUS—Emperor after the death of Petronius, 455-456. Deposed in a little over a year.

Avitus

MAJORIAN—Emperor after Avitus (457-461). Assassinated by one of his generals.

SEVERUS III—Emperor after Majorian (461-465). Poisoned by the same general who assassinated Majorian (Ricimer).

Majorian

RICIMER—A general in the Roman army who made and deposed (or executed) emperors. He was the real head of the government, but ruled it through others. He died in 472.

Severus III

ANTHEMIUS—A general in the eastern army. Proclaimed emperor by the Roman people, but assassinated by Ricimer. (467-472.)

Anthemius

Euphemia

EUPHEMIA—Wife of Anthemius.

OLYBRIUS—Son-in-law of Valentinian III. Sent to Italy to kill Ricimer, but Ricimer made him emperor. He died shortly thereafter. (472.)

Glycerius

GLYCERIUS—Emperor at Ravenna (473-474). Dethroned by Julius Nepos. Died a few years later.

Julius Nepos

JULIUS NEPOS—Emperor of the west after deposing Glycerius. Was deposed in 474 by Orestes, father of Romulus Augustulus, the last emperor of the west.

Romulus Augustulus

ROMULUS AUGUSTULUS—Last emperor of the west (475-476). Son of Orestes, but ruled in name only. Deposed by Odoacer, king of the Herculi. Retired and died at Campania.

The Use of the Inscription in Determining the Year a Coin Was Struck

A careful consideration of certain parts of the inscriptions on the coins of the empire, up until about the beginning of the third century, frequently will reveal the date that particular coin was struck.

The three most prominent means of such a determination are by;

1. The TR P
2. The COS
3. The IMP

It must be remembered, as explained elsewhere in this book, that the tribunician power was granted to the emperor for his lifetime, but that it was renewed annually. When it was so renewed each renewal would be indicated by the placing of a numeral after the TR P. Thus, TR P III would indicate that the coin was struck during the third year the emperor held such a title. Using a more specific example, a coin of the emperor Nerva upon which TR P II was inscribed would first indicate that the coin was struck during the second year he held the title. Using the chart which follows, it would be indicated that his second TR P was in the year 97. As further confirmation, and in order to deal with exceptions to this procedure, we would also examine the dates of his consulship and the dates, or years, in which he received the title Imperator by acclamation.

COS is the abbreviation of Consul. The emperor, most normally, served as one of the two consuls of the Roman state. Frequently, however, he designated another to serve in his stead. Inasmuch as any and all consulships were for one year only, and, further, inasmuch as the Romans used the

[101

same system of using numerals after the COS as they did with the TR P, it is often possible to determine the date of a coin by the COS. The outstanding difficulty in using the COS, by itself, however, lies in the aforementioned fact that quite frequently a period of years passed before an emperor would pick up the consulship again. A good example would be indicated in examining the consulships of the emperor Augustus. The chart shows us that he served his COS XI in the year 23 BC and his COS XII in 5 BC. As further demonstration, a coin of the emperor Vespasian bearing the title COS IIII (NOTE: Roman coins show the numeral four written as above, not as IV) could have been struck either in the year 72 or the year 73, for his COS V was not served until 74 and his COS III was served in the year 71. On the other hand, a coin of the emperor Domitian bearing COS X upon it would have had to have been struck in the year 84 because his COS VIIII was served in the year 83 and his COS XI was served in the year 85.

And yet a third means of finding the date of your coin may be found in the IMP part of the inscription. The IMP here referred to is that title which we have called the IMP by acclamation. It should be recalled that the emperor added numbers after this title, also, to designate extraordinary events, or victories in the field by his commanders. Thus, in examining a particular coin of the emperor Marcus Aurelius we find, as part of the inscription, the following: TR P XXIX, IMP VII, COS III. Studying the charts we find this information:

1. If his TR P II was in the year 147, his TR P XXIX occurred 27 years later, or in the year 174.

2. His third consulship (COS III) was served in the year 161. Apparently, we have a discrepancy, but careful observation will indicate that no more consulships appear upon the chart. The next step, then, is to turn to the IMP part of the inscription.

3. IMP VII appears in the chart under the year of 174. Our conclusion, then, is that the coin was struck in that year. The above example will indicate why it is necessary

to approach the charts from every possible angle before arriving at a conclusion. Occasionally, other titles might prove to be of some help, titles such as P P, CENSOR, or hereditary and honorary titles. However, too much faith should not be placed in the latter because of the generally extensive period covered by these titles.

In conclusion, it is necessary to say a word about the classification of the coins of the later empire, coins upon which practically none of the titles which we have been discussing appear. Such a classification requires knowledge far beyond the scope of this book, for here are involved questions of the subtle variances of style, of texture, of fabric, and other factors, complex and difficult. Quite frequently, the cultural background of the particular time in question must be studied and analyzed. In brief, it is a study in itself, a study which requires years of practice and effort.

The chart with TR P dates begins on page 120.

AUGUSTUS		TIBERIUS
COS XI	23 BC	
IMP VIIII	20 BC	
IMP X	15 BC	
	13 BC	COS
IMP XI	12 BC	
P M		
IMP XII	11 BC	
IMP XIII	9 BC	
IMP XIIII	8 BC	
	7 BC	COS II
COS XII	5 BC	
COS XIII	2 BC	
P P		
IMP XV	2 AD	
IMP XVI (?)	6 AD	
IMP XVII	6 AD	IMP III
IMP XVIII		IMP IIII
IMP XIX	9 AD	IMP V

AUGUSTUS	TIBERIUS
IMP XX..............11 AD...IMP VI	
12 AD...IMP VII	
IMP XXI.............14 AD...PRINCEPS	
15 AD...P M	
18 AD...COS III	
IMP VIII	
21 AD...COS IIII	
31 AD...COS V	

CALIGULA	CLAUDIUS
IMP.................37 AD	
P M	
COS	
P P..................38 AD	
COS II................39 AD	
COS III...............40 AD	
COS IIII..............41 AD...IMP	
IMP II	
IMP III	
IMP IIII	
P M	
42 AD...COS II	
P P	
43 AD...COS III	
44 AD...IMP V	
IMP VI	
IMP VII	
45 AD...IMP VIII	
46 AD...IMP VIIII	
IMP X	
IMP XI	
47 AD...COS IIII	
IMP XII	
IMP XIII	
48 AD...IMP XIIII	
IMP XV	

CLAUDIUS

48 AD...	CENSOR
49 AD...	IMP XVI
50 AD...	IMP XVII
	IMP XVIII
51 AD...	COS V
	IMP XXI
52 AD...	IMP XXIIII
53 AD...	IMP XXVII

NERO	GALBA: OTHO: VITELLIUS
IMP................54 AD	
P M	
COS................55 AD	
P P	
COS II..............57 AD	
IMP III	
COS III.............58 AD	
IMP IIII	
IMP V	
IMP VI.............59 AD	
COS IIII............60 AD	
IMP VII	
IMP VIII...........61 AD	
IMP VIIII	
IMP XI.............66 AD	
IMP XII............67 AD	
COS V..............68 AD...	IMP: P M (Galba)
	69 AD...COS II (Galba)
	69 AD...IMP: COS: P M (Otho)
	69 AD...IMP: GERM: COS (Vitellius)

VESPASIAN

IMP...................69 AD
IMP II

VESPASIAN

COS...................69 AD
P M
P P
COS II................70 AD
IMP III
IMP IIII
IMP V
COS III...............71 AD
IMP VI
IMP VII
IMP VIII
COS IIII..............72 AD
IMP X.................73 AD
COS V.................74 AD
IMP XI
IMP XII
COS VI................75 AD
IMP XIII
IMP XIIII
COS VII...............76 AD
IMP XV
IMP XVI
IMP XVII
IMP XVIII
COS VIII..............77 AD
IMP XIX...............78 AD
COS VIIII.............79 AD
IMP XX
AUG
P M

TITUS   DOMITIAN

COS...................70 AD
IMP...................71 AD...COS
IMP II
P M

TITUS	DOMITIAN
COS II.................72 AD	
IMP III	
CENSOR...............73 AD...COS II	
IMP IIII	
COS III................74 AD...COS III	
IMP VI	
IMP VII	
COS IIII...............75 AD	
IMP VII	
IMP VIII	
COS V.................76 AD...COS IIII	
IMP VIIII (?)	
IMP X (?)	
IMP XI	
IMP XII	
COS VI................77 AD...COS V	
IMP XIII..............78 AD	
COS VII...............79 AD...COS VI	
IMP XIIII	
IMP XV	
AUG	
P M	
P P	
COS VIII..............80 AD...COS VII	
IMP XVI..............81 AD...IMP	
IMP XVII	AUG
	P M
	P P
82 AD...COS VIII	
	IMP II
83 AD...COS VIIII	
	IMP III
	IMP IIII (?)
84 AD...COS X	
	IMP V
	IMP VI

DOMITIAN	NERVA

IMP VII	84 AD
GERM	
COS XI	85 AD
IMP VIII	
IMP VIIII	
IMP X	
IMP XI	
CENS PERPET	
COS XII	86 AD
IMP XII	
IMP XIII	
IMP XIIII	
COS XIII	87 AD
COS XIIII	88 AD
IMP XV	
IMP XVI	
IMP XVII	
IMP XVIII	
IMP XIX	
IMP XX	
IMP XXI	
COS XV	90 AD
COS XVI	92 AD
COS XVII	95 AD

	96 AD	COS II
		IMP
		CAES
		AUG
	97 AD...	COS III
		IMP II
		GERM
	98 AD...	COS IIII

TRAJAN	

CAES	97 AD
IMP	

TRAJAN	HADRIAN

GERM..................97 AD	
COS II.................98 AD	
AUG	
P M	
P P	
COS III...............100 AD	
COS IIII..............101 AD	
IMP II	
IMP III...............102 AD	
IMP IIII	
COS V................103 AD	
IMP V................105 AD	
IMP VI...............106 AD	
COS VI...............112 AD	
OPTIMUS.............114 AD	
IMP VIII.............115 AD	
IMP VIIII	
IMP X	
IMP XI	
IMP XII	
IMP XIII (?)	
PARTHICUS..........116 AD	
	117 AD...COS
	IMP
	CAES
	AUG
	P M
	P P
	118 AD...COS II
	119 AD...COS III
	128 AD...P P
	135 AD...IMP II

AELIUS

COS...................136 AD
CAES

AELIUS	**ANTONINUS PIUS**
P M.................136 AD	
COS II...............137 AD	
	138 AD...COS
	CAES
	IMP
	AUG
	P M
	PIUS
	COS DES II
	139 AD...COS II
	COS DES III
	IMP II
	P P
	140 AD...COS III
	144 AD...COS DES IIII
	145 AD...COS IIII

MARCUS AURELIUS	**LUCIUS VERUS**
CAES.................139 AD	
COS DES	
COS..................140 AD	
COS DES II...........144 AD	
COS II...............145 AD	
P M..................147 AD...CAES	
	154 AD...COS
COS III..............161 AD...COS II	
IMP	IMP
AUG	AUG
	P M
IMP II...............163 AD...IMP II:	
	ARMENIACUS
ARMENIACUS..........164 AD	
IMP III..............165 AD...IMP III: PARTHICUS	
MEDICUS.............166 AD...MEDICUS	
PARTHICUS	IMP IIII
IMP IIII	

MARCUS AURELIUS	LUCIUS VERUS
P P..................167 AD	...COS III
	P P
IMP V................168 AD	...IMP V
IMP VI...............171 AD	
GERM................172 AD	
IMP VII..............174 AD	
SARMATICUS.........175 AD	
IMP VIII	
IMP VIIII............177 AD	
IMP X...............179 AD	

COMMODUS

CAES.................166 AD
GERM................172 AD
SARMATICUS.........175 AD
IMP..................176 AD
COS..................177 AD
IMP II
AUG
P P
IMP III...............179 AD
COS II
IMP IIII..............180 AD
COS III...............181 AD
IMP V................182 AD
COS IIII..............183 AD
IMP VI
PIUS
P M
IMP VII..............184 AD
BRITTANICUS
FELIX................185 AD
COS V................186 AD
IMP VIII
COS VI...............190 AD

[111

COMMODUS	PERTINAX: DIDIUS JULIANUS: CLODIUS ALBINUS:
COS VII..............192 AD	...COS II (Pertinax)
	193 AD...IMP: AUG: P M: P P (Pertinax)
	193 AD...IMP: CAES: AUG (Didius)
	193 AD...COS: (Clodius)
	194 AD...COS II (Clodius)

SEPTIMIUS SEVERUS	CARACALLA
COS...................193 AD	
IMP	
CAES	
AUG	
P M	
P P	
COS II...............194 AD	
IMP II	
IMP III	
IMP IIII	
PIUS..................195 AD	
PARTHICUS	
ARABICUS	
ADIABENICUS	
IMP V	
IMP VI	
IMP VII	
IMP VIII..............196 AD	...CAES
IMP VIIII.............197 AD	...P M
IMP X	
IMP XI...............198 AD	...IMP
	AUG
201 AD	...PIUS
	FELIX
	PARTHICUS

SEPTIMIUS SEVERUS	CARACALLA
COS III . . . . 202 AD	. . . COS
	205 AD . . . COS II
	207 AD . . . IMP II
	208 AD . . . COS III
	P P
BRITTANICUS . . . . 209 AD	
IMP XV	
	210 AD . . . BRITTANICUS
	211 AD . . . P M

CARACALLA	GETA
	198 AD . . . CAES
	205 AD . . . COS
	208 AD . . . COS II
	209 AD . . . AUG
	PIUS
	210 AD . . . BRITTANICUS
	211 AD . . . IMP
	P P
COS IIII . . . . 213 AD	
GERM	
IMP III	
INVICTUS	
IMP IIII . . . . 214 AD	

MACRINUS: DIADUMENIANUS	ELAGABALUS
IMP: CAES: AUG: P M:	
P P (Macrinus) . . . . 217 AD	
CAES (Diadumenianus) . 217 AD	
COS II (Macrinus) . . . . . 218 AD	. . . IMP
IMP: AUG (Diadumenianus)	CAES
	COS
	AUG
	P M
	P P

[113

	ELAGABALUS
	219 AD...COS II
	220 AD...COS III
	222 AD...COS IIII

SEVERUS ALEXANDER	MAXIMINUS
CAES.................221 AD	
P M	
COS..................222 AD	
IMP	
AUG	
P P	
COS II...............226 AD	
COS III..............229 AD	
	235 AD...IMP
	CAES
	AUG
	P M
	P P
	236 AD...GERM
	IMP III
	IMP IIII
	237 AD...IMP V
	IMP VI
	238 AD...IMP VII

GORDIANUS I	
GORDIANUS II	BALBINUS
IMP: CAES: AUG: P M	
P P (Gordianus I)......238 AD...IMP: CAES: AUG: P M	
IMP: CAES: AUG: P M	
(Gordianus II).........238 AD	

PUPIENUS	GORDIANUS PIUS III
CAES.................235 AD	
GERM................238 AD...CAES	
SARMATICUS	AUG
DACICUS	IMP

PUPIENUS		**GORDIANUS PIUS III**
IMP	238 AD	P M
AUG		P P
P M		
P P		
	239 AD	COS
	240 AD	IMP II
		IMP III
	241 AD	COS II
	242 AD	IMP VI

PHILLIP I		**PHILLIP II**
IMP	244 AD	NOB C
CAES		
AUG		
P P		
P M		
PARTHICUS		
PERSICUS		
COS	245 AD	
	246 AD	AUG
COS II	247 AD	IMP
		CAES
		AUG
		P M
		P P
COS III	248 AD	COS II
CARPICUS		CARPICUS
GERM		GERM

TRAJAN DECIUS:
HERRENIUS ETRUSCUS:
HOSTILLIANUS

IMP: CAES: AUG: P M: 249 AD
P P (Decius)
COS II (Decius)........250 AD
CAES (Herrenius)......250 AD
CAES (Hostillianus).....250 AD

TRAJAN DECIUS: HERRENIUS ETRUSCUS: HOSTILLIANUS	TREBONIANUS GALLUS: VOLUSIAN: AEMILIANUS
AUG (Hostillianus)......250 AD	
COS III (Decius).......251 AD	
DACICUS (Decius)	
COS: AUG (Herrenius)..251 AD...	IMP: CAES: AUG: P M: P P (Trebonianus)
	251 AD...CAES: AUG: P M: P P: (Volusian)
	252 AD...COS II (Trebonianus)
	252 AD...COS (Volusian)
	253 AD...COS II (Volusian)
	253 AD...IMP: CAES: AUG: (Aemilianus)

VALERIANUS	GALLIENUS
IMP..................253 AD...	IMP
CAES	CAES
AUG	AUG
P M	P M
P P	P P
COS	
COS II...............254 AD...	COS
IMP VII	
COS III..............255 AD...	COS II
	256 AD...IMP III
	DACICUS
COS IIII.............257 AD...	COS III

POSTUMUS	
IMP..................258 AD	
CAES	
AUG	
P M	
P P	
COS..................259 AD	

POSTUMUS	GALLIENUS
COS II..............260 AD	
COS III.............261 AD	...COS IIII
	IMP X
	262 AD...COS V
	264 AD...COS VI
	266 AD...COS VII
COS IIII............267 AD	
COS V..............268 AD	

CLAUDIUS II:	AURELIAN:
TETRICUS:	TACITUS:
MARIUS:	FLORIANUS:
QUINTILLUS	PROBUS

IMP:CAES:AUG:P M: 268 AD
P P (Claudius)
COS: IMP: CAES: AUG:
P M: P P (Tetricus)....268 AD
IMP: CAES: AUG:
(Marius)..............268 AD
IMP: CAES: AUG:
(Quintillus)............269 AD
       270(?)AD..IMP: CAES: AUG:
            (Aurelian)
       271 AD...COS (Aurelian)
       274 AD...COS II (Aurelian)
       275 AD...COS III (Aurelian)
       275 AD...IMP: CAES: AUG:
           P M: COS DES II:
           P P (Tacitus)
       276 AD...COS II (Tacitus)
       276 AD...IMP: CAES: AUG
           (Florianus)
       276 AD...IMP: CAES: AUG:
           P P: P M (Probus)
       277 AD...COS (Probus)
       278 AD...COS II (Probus)

PROBUS

279 AD...COS III (Probus)
281 AD...COS IIII (Probus)
282 AD...COS V (Probus)

CARUS: CARINUS: NUMERIAN: DIOCLETIAN	MAXIMIANUS: CONSTANTIUS: GALERIUS
IMP: CAES: AUG: P M: 282 AD P P (Carus)	
CAES (Carinus)........282 AD	
CAES (Numerian)......282 AD	
COS II (Carus)........283 AD	
AUG: COS: IMP: P M: P P (Carinus)..........283 AD	
AUG: IMP: COS: PP: (Numerian).............283 AD	
COS II (Carinus).......284 AD	
COS II (Numerian).....284 AD	
IMP: CAES: COS: AUG: P M: P P (Diocletian)..284 AD	
COS III (Carinus)......285 AD	
COS II (Diocletian).....285 AD	...CAES (Maximianus)
	286 AD...AUG: P M: P P: IMP: CAES: (Maximianus)
COS III (Diocletian)....287 AD	...COS (Maximianus)
	288 AD...COS II (Maximianus)
COS IIII (Diocletian)...290 AD	...COS III (Maximianus)
	292 AD...COS: CAES (Constantius)
	292 AD...COS: CAES (Galerius)
COS V (Diocletian).....293 AD	...COS IIII (Maximianus)
IMP X (Diocletian).....294 AD	...IMP VIIII (Maximianus)
COS VI (Diocletian)....296 AD	...COS II (Constantius)

DIOCLETIAN	MAXIMIANUS: CONSTANTIUS: GALERIUS
	297 AD...COS V (Maximianus)
	297 AD...COS II (Galerius)
COS VII (Diocletian)...	299 AD...COS VI (Maximianus)
	300 AD...COS III (Constantius)
	300 AD...COS III (Galerius)
IMP XVIII (Diocletian)	301 AD...IMP VII (Maximianus)
	302 AD...COS IIII (Constantius)
	302 AD...COS IIII (Galerius)
COS VIII (Diocletian)...	303 AD...COS VII (Maximianus)
COS VIIII (Diocletian)..	304 AD...COS VIII (Maximianus)
	305 AD...COS V (Constantius)
	305 AD...COS V (Galerius)
	305 AD...IMP: AUG: P M: P P (Constantius and Galerius)

Dates of the Tribunicia Potestas (Tribunician Power) of the Emperors

(TR P)

AUGUSTUS
TR P, June 27, 23 BC. TR P II, same day and month, 22 BC, and renewed annually on the same date. Thus, at his death in 14 AD he was in the course of his TR P XXXVII.

TIBERIUS
TR P, June 27, 6 BC. Renewed annually until TR P V in 2 BC. TR P VI not until June 27, 4 AD. In order to find the year Anno Domini, deduct 2 from the TR P (thus, TR P XXX would be in the year 28 AD, or really, 28-29 AD, because it was renewed in June of each year and ran to June of the next year).

CALIGULA
TR P, March 18, 37 AD. Renewed annually on the same date in the years 38, 39 and 40.

CLAUDIUS I
TR P, January 25, 41 AD. Renewed annually on that date. At his death in 54 AD, he was in the course of his TR P XIIII.

NERO
TR P, October 13, 54 AD. Renewed annually on that date until 59 AD, when he apparently started a new system by shortening his TR P VI and counting, thereafter, from December 4 (or 10th?), when he took TR P VII and renewed annually on that date. At his death in June, 68, he was in the course of TR P XIIII.

GALBA
TR P, only.

OTHO
TR P, only.

VITELLIUS
TR P, only.

VESPASIAN
TR P, July 1, 69. Renewed annually on the same date. At his death in June, 79, he was in the course of his TR P X.

TITUS
TR P, July 1, 71. Renewed annually on the same date. At his death in September, 81, he was in the course of his TR P XII.

DOMITIAN
TR P, September 13, 81. Renewed annually on the same date. At his death in September, 96, he was in the course of his TR P XVI.

NERVA
TR P, September 18, 96. TR P II from the same date in the year 97. Apparently started TR P III in December of the same year (97). However, some inscriptions, particularly those which are found upon monuments, fail to recognize a TR P III and carry the TR P II to his death on January 25, 98.

TRAJAN
TR P, October 27, 97. TR P II from December 10, 97. Renewed annually on the latter date. At his death in August, 117, he was in the course of his TR P XXI.

HADRIAN
TR P from the death of Trajan in August, 117. TR P II from December 10, 117. Renewed annually on the latter date. At his death on July 10, 138, he was in the course of his TR P XXII.

ANTONINUS PIUS
TR P, February 25, 138. TR P II, December 10, 138, and renewed annually on the latter date. At his death in March, 161, he was in the course of his TR P XXIIII.

MARCUS AURELIUS
TR P, Feruary 25, 147. TR P II, December 10, 147. Renewed annually on the latter date. At his death in March, 180, he was in the course of his TR P XXXIIII.

LUCIUS VERUS
TR P, March 7, 161. TR P II, December 10, 161, and renewed annually on the latter date. At his death in the winter of 169 he was in the course of his TR P VIIII.

COMMODUS
TR P, November 27, 176. TR P II, December 10, 176, and renewed annually on the latter date. At his death in December, 192, he was in the course of his TR P XVIII.

PERTINAX
TR P, only.

DIDIUS JULIANUS
TR P, only.

SEPTIMIUS SEVERUS
TR P, June 1, 193. TR P II, December 10, 193. Renewed annually on the latter date. At his death in February, 211, he was in the course of his TR P XVIIII.

CARACALLA
TR P, June 2, 198. TR P II, December 10, 198, and renewed annually on the latter date. At his death in April (or March?), 217, he was in the course of TR P XX.

GETA
TR P, sometime in 209. TR P II, December 10, 209, renewed annually on the latter date. At his death in April, 212, he was in the course of his TR P IIII.

MACRINUS
TR P, April 11, 217 to January, 218(?). TR P II from latter date to June 8, 218, which was the date of his death.

ELAGABALUS
TR P, 218. Renewed annually each year until his death in 222 when he was in the course of TR P V.

SEVERUS ALEXANDER
TR P, March 11, 222. Renewed annually, apparently in January of each year. At his death in 235 he was in the course of TR P XIIII.

MAXIMINUS
TR P, 235. TR P II, 236. TR P III, 237 (January 16?), TR P IIII, 238 (January 16?).

GORDIANUS I
TR P, only.

GORDIANUS II
TR P, only.

BALBINUS
TR P, only.

PUPIENUS
TR P, only.

GORDIANUS III (PIUS)
TR P, 238. Renewed annually. At his death in 244, he was in the course of TR P VII.

PHILIPPUS I
TR P, March, 244. TR P II, January, 245. Renewed annually until his death in September or October, 249.

TRAJAN DECIUS
Apparently two methods employed here. Either:
1. When saluted emperor by the troops in 248, or
2. From the death of Philippus in September or October, 249. He died in 251.

HERRENNIUS ETRUSCUS
TR P in 250. Died, November, 251.

HOSTILIANUS
TR P in 250. Died, December, 251.

TREBONIANUS GALLUS
Uncertain TR P. Probably November or December, 251. TR P II, 252. TR P IIII (not III), in 253.

VOLUSIANUS
Same as his father, Trebonianus Gallus.

VALERIANUS AND GALLIENUS
TR P dates are the same for both (father and son). TR P, 253. TR P II, 254. TR P III, 255. Valerian was in the course of TR P VII at his death in 259. Gallienus was in the course of TR P XVI at his death in 268.

POSTUMUS
TR P, 258. TR P II, 259. Renewed annually until his death in 267, when he was in the course of TR P X.

CLAUDIUS II
TR P, 268. Renewed annually. At his death in 270 he was in the course of TR P III.

TETRICUS I
TR P, 270. Renewed annually. At his abdication in 273 he was in the course of TR P III.

AURELIAN
TR P, 270. Renewed annually. At his death in 275 he was in the course of TR P VI.

TACITUS
TR P, September 25, 275. TR P II, January 1, 276.

PROBUS
TR P, probably in 276. Renewed annually. At his death in 282 he was in the course of TR P VII.

CARUS
TR P, 282. TRP II, 283.

CARINUS
TR P, 282. Renewed annually. At his death in 285 he was in the course of TR P III.

NUMERIANUS
TR P, 283, TR P II, 284.

DIOCLETIAN
TR P, September 17, 284. TR P II, March 1(?), 285, and renewed annually on the latter date. At his abdication in March, 305, he was in the course of TR P XXII.

MAXIMIAN
Counted his TR P from 285, so that he was always one behind Diocletian (above).

NOTE: The Tribunician power was not assumed by Constantius or Galerius.

BIBLIOGRAPHY

Space will not permit the inclusion of all the fine books and papers on the subject of Roman coins. Those listed here are some of the standard reference works on the subject. The reader will notice that I have not only listed books about the coinage, but also about Roman history.

BOOKS OF THE ROMAN REPUBLIC

BABELON, E. "Description historique et chronologique des monnaies la Republique romain." (Paris, 1885-86) Reprint, Bologna, 1963
GRANT, M. "From Imperium to Auctoritas" (Cambridge, 1946)
GRUEBER, H. A. "Coins of the Roman Republic in the British Museum" (London, 1910) Reprint, London, 1970.
MATTINGLY, H. "Roman Coins" (Quadrangle, 1960)
PINK, K. "The triumviri Monetales and the Structure of the Coinage of the Roman Republic" (The American Numismatic Society. Numismatic Studies No. 7. 1952)
SEABY, H. A. "Roman Silver Coins" (London, 1967)
SEAR, D. "Roman Coins and their Values" (London, 1970)
STEVENSON, C. H. V. "A Dictionary of Roman Coins" (London, 1889) Reprinted, London, 1964
SYDENHAM, E. A. "The Roman Republican Coinage" (London, 1952) Reprint, New York, 1976

BOOKS OF THE ROMAN EMPIRE

COHEN, H. "Description historique des monnais frapées sous l'Empire romain" (1880-92). Reprint, Graz, 1965
MATTINGLY, H. A. "Roman Coins" (Quadrangle, 1960)
MATTINGLY, H. A. "Coins of the Roman Empire in the British Museum" (1923-1940) Reprints, 1962-1968, London.
SEABY, H. A. "Roman Silver Coins"
  Vol. I, London, 1967; Republic-Augustus.
  Vol. II, London, 1968; Tiberius-Commodus.
  Vol. III, London, 1969; Pertinax-Balbinus and Pupienus.
  Vol. IV, London, 1971; Gordian III- Postumus.
SEAR, D. "Roman Coins and their Values" (London, 1970)
STEVENSON, C. H. V. "Dictionary of Roman Coins" London, 1889 Reprint, London, 1964

A FEW BOOKS ON ROMAN HISTORY

GIBBON, "The Decline and Fall of the Roman Empire"
MOMMSEN, "The History of Rome"
PLUTARCH, "The Lives of the Noble Grecians and Romans" (popularly called, "Lives")
SEUTONIUS, "The Lives of the Twelve Caesars"
TACITUS, "Annals and History"

INDEX

	Page
Abundantia	44
Aelia Flaccilla	96
Aelius	70, 109
Aemilian	81, 116
Aequitas	44
Aesculapius	38
Aeternitas	44
Agrippa	62
Agrippina the Elder	64
Agrippina the Younger	65
Alexander	90
Allectus	88
Annia Faustina	75
Annius Verus	71
Annona	44
Anthemius	99
Antonia	63
Antoninus Pius	70, 110, 121
Apollo	38
Aquilia Severa	75
Arcadius	97
Augustus	62, 103, 120
Aurelian	85, 117, 124
Avitus	99
Balbinus	78, 114, 123
Bonus Eventus	45
Brittanicus	65
Caesonia	65
Caius Caesar	63
Caligula	64, 104, 120
Caracalla	74, 112, 122
Carausius	88
Carinus	87, 118, 124
Carus	86, 118, 124
Ceres	38
Claudius	65, 104, 120
Claudius II (Gothicus)	84, 117, 124
Clementia	45
Clodius Albinus	73, 112
Clodius Macer	66
Commodus	72, 111, 122
Concordia	45
Constans	93
Constantine I (The Great)	91
Constantine II	92
Constantine III	97
Constantius I (Chlorus)	89, 118
Constantius II	93
Constantius Gallus	93
Constantius III	97
Cornelia Supera	81

	Page
Crispina	72
Crispus	92
Cybele	38
Decentius	94
Delmatius	92
Diadumenian	75, 113
Diana	39
Didia Clara	73
Didius Julianus	72, 112, 122
Diocletian	88, 118, 124
Domitian	68, 106, 121
Domitilla	67
Drusilla	65
Drusus Caesar	64
Drusus Junior	63
Dryantilla	83
Elagabalus	75, 113, 122
Etruscilla	80
Eugenius	96
Euphemia	100
Fausta	92
Faustina the Elder	70
Faustina the Younger	71
Felicitas	45
Fides	45
Flavius Victor	96
Florianus	86, 117
Fortuna	46
Galba	66, 105, 120
Galeria Valeria	89
Galerius	89, 118
Galla Placida	97
Gallienus	82, 116, 124
Germanicus	64
Geta	74, 113, 122
Glycerius	100
Gordianus Africanus I	77, 114, 123
Gordianus Africanus II	78, 114, 123
Gordianus III (Pius)	78, 114, 123
Gratian	95
Hadrian	69, 109, 121
Hanniballianus	92
Helena	89, 94
Heliogabalus (See Elagabalus)	
Hercules	39
Herrenius Etruscus	80, 115, 123
Hilaritas	46
Honorius	97

INDEX—Continued

Honos	46
Hostilian	80, 115, 123
Indulgentia	46
Janus	39
Johannes	98
Jotapian	79
Jovian	94
Jovinus	98
Julia	62
Julia Domna	73
Julia Maesa	76
Julia Mamaea	77
Julia Paula	75
Julia Soaemias	76
Julia Titi	68
Julian	87
Julian II	94
Julius Nepos	100
Juno	40
Jupiter	39
Justitia	47
Laetitia	47
Laelianus	84
Liber	40
Liberalitas	47
Libertas	47
Licinia Eudoxia	99
Licinius I	90
Licinius II	91
Livia	62
Lucilla	71
Lucius Caesar	63
Lucius Verus	71, 110, 122
Macrianus I	83
Macrianus II	83
Macrinus	74, 113, 122
Magnentius	94
Magnia Urbica	87
Magnus Maximus	96
Majorian	99
Manlia Scantilla	72
Marciana	69
Marcus Aurelius	71, 110, 122
Mariniana	82
Marius	84, 117
Mars	40
Martinian	91
Matidia	69
Maxentius	90
Maximianus I (Herculius)	88, 118, 124
Maximinus I	77, 114, 123
Maximinus II (Daza)	90
Maximus	98
Mercury	41
Minerva	41
Moneta	48
Nepotian	93
Neptune	41
Nero	66, 105, 120
Nero Caesar	64
Nero Claudius Drusus	63
Nerva	68, 108, 121
Nigrinian	87
Numerian	87, 118, 124
Olybrius	100
Orbiana	76
Otacilia Severa	79
Otho	67, 105, 121
Pacatian	79
Patientia	48
Paulina	77
Pax	48
Pertinax	72, 112, 122
Pescennius Niger	73
Petronius Maximus	99
Philip I	79, 115, 123
Philip II	79, 115
Pietas	48
Plautilla	74
Plotina	69
Poppaea	66
Postumus	83, 116, 124
Priscus Attalus	98
Probus	86, 117, 124
Procopius	95
Providentia	49
Pudicitia	49
Pupienus	78, 114, 123
Quietus	83
Quintillus	85, 117
Regalianus	83
Ricimer	99
Roma	42
Romulus	90
Romulus Augustulus	100
Sabina	70
Salonina	82
Saloninus	82
Salus	49
Sebastianus	98

INDEX—*Continued*

	Page
Securitas	49
Septimius Severus	73, 112, 122
Severina	85
Severus Alexander	76, 114, 123
Severus II	89
Severus III	99
Sol	42
Spes	50
Tacitus	86, 117, 124
Tetricus I	84, 117, 124
Tetricus II	84
Theodosius I (The Great)	96
Theodora	91
Three Graces	43
Tiberius	63, 103, 120
Titus	68, 106, 121
Trajan	69, 108, 121
Trajan Decius	80, 115, 123
Tranquillina	79
Trebonianus Gallus	80, 116, 123

	Page
Uberitas	50
Uranius Antoninus	77
Vabalathus	85
Valens	91, 95
Valentinian I	95
Valentinian II	95
Valentinian III	98
Valerian	81, 116, 124
Valerian II	82
Venus	42
Vespasian	67, 105, 121
Vesta	42
Vetranio	93
Victoria	50
Victorinus	84
Virtus	50
Vitellius	67, 105, 121
Volusian	81, 116
Vulcan	43
Zenobia	85